WRITE HOME

Letters to a Younger Me

WRITE HOME

Letters to a Younger Me

Edited by Shannon Ivey and Melanie McGehee

A Communal Pen Workshop Anthology

athenaeum
PRESS
AT COASTAL CAROLINA UNIVERSITY

The Athenaeum Press at Coastal Carolina University
Edwards College of Humanities and Fine Arts
PO Box 261954, Conway, SC 25928

Printed in the United States.

Cover Design: Anna Brown
Interior Design: Kendall Boykin
Press Editor: Lilith Yurkin

Identifiers: LCCN: 2026939693 | ISBN: 9781970030174

Communal Pen showcases short stories to explore the dynamic and ever-changing state of South Carolina. We create space for, amplify, and connect the state's diverse voices through writing workshops, publications, and a digital platform. This work was completed with the What She Said project.

Communal Pen is supported through a partnership with the SC Arts Commission, which recieves funding from the National Endowment for the Arts.

Contents

Letters of Witness to the Past

Letters of Witness to the Present

Letters of Reclamation

Letters of Release

Letters of Celebration

Post Script

Dear Reader,

We are glad you are here. You are about to become an important part of this work. After all, an anthology needs readers.

You're holding a love project that has been brewing for over a decade. The #whatshesaidproject started as a storytelling initiative in Columbia, SC. During the pandemic, it grew to be a podcast. And next, it became a teaching and learning space for folks who wanted to write and tell their life stories.

In May of 2025, Melanie McGehee and I attended a publishing symposium in upstate South Carolina, and played hooky on the second day of the conference to plan our next steps. Those steps were clear: we wanted to hold workshops where people could practice writing letters to their younger selves and then publish them in an anthology.

Had we ever published an anthology? No. But with our collective experiences (Melanie with her MFA in Creative Writing and me with my MFA in Theatre and event producing background), we believed that we could figure it out. I then came up with the title "Write Home," but none of that really matters, as I cannot see this project without us both in it.

Next, we needed a publishing partner, and as we had both had great experiences with the Athenaeum Press at Coastal Carolina and their Communal Pen writing workshops over the last several years, we brought our idea to them. It was a fast yes, and we could not be more happy about the process and collaboration.

During the fall months of 2025, our writers wrote first for themselves, using the structure of a letter. But they also wrote for you. Some of them have never been published, and others are professional writers. Their backgrounds were not important to us, but their ability to hold vulnerability and wisdom at the same time was. We didn't predetermine this book's structure, but you will find that the categories we found for the selected submissions are quite natural.

May this book remind you that you are important, every version of you, and that your stories are special. We believe that telling and receiving these stories reminds us of our shared humanity and broadens our capacity for empathy—for ourselves and others.

And what better time to create this literary love bomb than now?

Thank you for being here. It matters.

Shannon Ivey

Letters of Blessing

If only you knew how special you are.

-Triston Dabney

Triston Dabney

My Dearest,

I am older now
becoming all the things
I swore I'd never be.
I've gargled
the gravel of sorrow,
danced in full fat,
tugged at the skirts
of uninvited thoughts—

become someone's hero
and then
disappointed them.

I became like my dad—
though I was never fair to him—
and I've surrendered
much of existence
to the wholeness
of change.

Young one, hear this:
if you've ever
found yourself
living
even if for a moment

hallowed by self-doubt

then you, my dearest—
a vessel
of silica
and beatitudes

have gone
and prepared
a place for love.

You have simply
done the greatest growing
of all.

You've given your bones
a tuning fork
to find their eponymous tone.

These aches you felt
were just the chimes
of your soul
leaving the porch light on—

calling yourself
back home.

Triston Dabney (he/him) is a poet, cultural worker, and Oprah Winfrey Scholar from Baltimore, Maryland with a BA in English Literature. Triston has received scholarships and support from Stockton University, Sphinx Moth Press, and the Hudson Valley Writers Center and is a Pushcart and Best of the Net Nominee. His work appears in Obsidian, BreakBread Magazine, The Elevation Review, *and other literary spaces committed to Black and queer poetics.*

His debut poetry collection, Moments as They Are *(Fernwood Press, 2026), traces a journey through boyhood, memory, spirituality, and becoming with lyrical precision and radical tenderness.*

V. Rendina

To [the thirteen-year-old kid crawling inside their skin],

They have a name for how it feels to live inside our body, we just need to live long enough to learn it. We do not need to shrink ourselves for safety. We do not need to slump our shoulders to hide the chest we hate. No more Ace bandage binds beneath sports bras, and, frankly, it's a good thing we quit that while we were ahead. We spared ourselves some damage, though you and I both know improper binding was the least of the damage we inflicted.

I'm not saying shit gets easy. Some days the home we return to welcomes us with warmth from wall to wall. Sometimes, we wonder who trashed this so-called temple with graffiti scars and broken bottles and litter left to rot along the floorboards. But we learn to live within ourselves, regardless of the mess we made. It just takes time.

And when we learn who we are, we wear the word with pride. Some days. The future is foreign like that. Unfamiliar with its pearl-clutching, with its false hope for forward movement while we spiral back ten thousand steps. Yet the word, that name that defines how it feels to feel within our body. The relief it gives us lasts for lifetimes. We find ourselves within this name. We find friends who share our identity. Who know what it's like to live inside this wreckage. And that singer you love in that band, the one mom hopes is just a phase.[1] I know how badly you wish to look like him. Turns out he suffers from the same discomfort. And lives long enough to speak on his experience, too. So, hang in there. The people we meet will make the pain subside. Once your present becomes our past. No matter what the future says.

So much has changed since I lived as this version of you. I wish it was all for the best. I wish I could tell you what you need to hear. But we've read too many books about time travel, about messing

---

1 Don't worry, the band was never just a phase. We still love those sad songs for how many times they helped us survive. Mom gets it in due time.

with the future from the slightest mistake we make in the past. So, I can't spoil too much of your road ahead. Can't share our secrets with you like gossip. I can tell you we still write your weird stories. About werewolves, and witches, and monsters that make us feel most home in our body. We don't really like the lady who inspired us to write anymore, but that's a long story. One that definitely fucks with the timeline, should I spill the beans. The good news is our love of writing comes from within us in due time. We make our own monsters from the real ones we overcome. We find comfort in ourselves from the words we write. And every time I write, I still think of your commitment to the craft. How little you cared about perfection, so long as you got the story out of your head. So long as you told the story you longed to tell inside your heart. I try to write like you each day. If only to remind me where we started. If only to keep your weird kid legacy[2] alive.

I have to wonder if I've told you too much. Maybe this letter is why the future's not so bright. Why it's fine for us to feel peace within our skin, while the rest of the world wages war against our pride. Maybe I'm giving us too much credit to changing the cosmic threads of this reality. Or maybe we do matter, because we matter, no matter how small this letter impacts the future. But I know I shouldn't even share the name that saves your life. The name, unfortunately, just doesn't exist in your time. But the identity is real. The sensations are real. The way we feel has existed for centuries. And the day will come when you finally hear what word to call yourself. What identity describes what it's like to live with a mind that sees ourselves beyond the binary box the world wants to cram us into.

And when we finally figure ourselves out, I promise it's worth the wait.

Let's make a deal. You give yourself at least a decade. Then a decade after that. Within that time, you'll find yourself. And when you do, I'll match each decade you gift us for years and years to come.

So live for me, would you?

---

2 Contrary to popular belief, it's cool to be a weird kid in the future, just trust me.

Live long enough for both of us to experience some joy.

xo,

[the version of you still alive in twenty years' time]

V. Rendina (they/them) is a queer writer from Northeastern Pennsylvania. V. earned their MFA in Creative Writing from Wilkes University in January 2025, where they received the Norris Church Mailer Scholarship for excellence in writing. Their work has been longlisted for Uncharted Magazine, and their short story "To Shun the Light of Day" is forthcoming in Fantasy & Science Fiction Magazine. For updates, you can find V. Rendina on all social media platforms @vrendinawrites.

Charlie Hebert-Russell

You will ...

You will dream with your heart. You will be young and in love and feel it amplified in your life and in your womb. You will feel so much possibility, so much promise, so much happiness that you question your plans and purpose, wondering if it is too good to be true. You will survive.

You will feel the soul-wrenching, gut-clenching, bone-crushing void—the emptiness of womb and home as your big dreams gain tiny wings. You will survive.

You will stand zombie-like and untethered, toes on the cliff overlooking the abyss, ready to fall forward with abandon, regret, defeat. You will survive.

You will find new purpose, new dreams, new fullness as your body grows along with a new human, as your family grows over and over. Your time will be busy. Your house will be lived in. Your heart will expand until you think it might explode. You will survive.

You will build a home and plan out your years, only to have it destroyed by a disaster that's anything but natural. You will pick up your family and move to a new town where you know no one, grieving and running to keep up with life as it moves on. You will survive.

Your home will fill with laughter and chaos. You will lose sleep holding a sick child. You will step on Lego pieces and doll shoes strewn like landmines in your field of dreams. You will build forts for movie nights and weather the seasons from stadium bleachers. You will try to capture each moment—documenting, holding, remembering—but you are not fast enough to hold down the present while saving space for the future.

You will drive hundreds of miles, chauffeur and co-pilot, following their haphazard map of what-ifs and maybes toward dreams of their own. You will rent U-Hauls to move the boxes of their youth to new places where they will raise their own. You will watch your heart grow smaller in the rearview mirror, leaving the biggest and best part of you behind. You will survive.

You will stand on aching feet cooking for the growing brood on holidays, stowing some away for late-night pantry raids. You will lie in bed caught between memory and now, listening to giggles as they "sneak" to fill their ever-growing bellies without waking you. You will smile, knowing these times won't last.

You will wish them back during sleepless nights when the clock down the hall ticks so loudly it echoes in your ears, when there is nothing but silence—reminders of your empty nest. You will survive.

You will counsel them, hold them, marvel at them. Your heart will be ripped from your chest as you witness their mistakes and great accomplishments, embarrassment and defeat, true love and heartbreak, birth and death—the moments they believe they will not survive. You will be there to remind them that they will.

You will want to take their pain, to fix it. You can't—and shouldn't. It's theirs to journey through. So you watch, hold their hand, feed them, cheer for them, pray for them. You will survive.

You will love deeply, completely, messily, with mistakes and misunderstandings. You will hurt them. They will hurt you. You will still love unconditionally, without regret. They will leave. You will feel lost, unsure of who you are, what you should do, or who you want to be. You will survive.

You will see your mother in the mirror one day. When you smile, she smiles back. Her gray is now yours—strange, yet comforting. Until you wake inside a stranger's body, willing it to move, its laughter echoing in your bones, reminders of mortality. You will survive.

You won't believe me. You will scream and cry, suffer in silence, try to fix it all, blame yourself, search for answers, pray it's the last time. You will be certain this moment will take you out, unable to see the other side or know that even as you cry in your closet, you are already moving through it—the fog, the darkness, the uncertainty, all the emotions that come with it.

You won't know it then, but you will survive.

How do I know? Because you're here—worn and weathered, wise and strong, slow and gray, experienced, grateful, loved. Alive.

Charlie Hebert-Russell (she/her)—educator, massage therapist, and village mom—writes from south Mississippi, where salt air, strong women, and a lifetime of doing-what-needs-to-be-done have shaped her voice. Her writing blends decades of love, loss, and watching people grow, fall apart, rebuild, and try again. A quiet and practical soul, Charlie has long been the person people call when something needs fixing, explaining, or calming down. Her belief is that every experience—even the difficult ones—becomes material for growth, understanding, and legacy.

Dory Maguire

Letter to My Childhood Self

Thinking about
what to say to you,
and how to say it,
I took a walk
along the water
to clear my head.
I picked up a pebble
that once had been clay,
which encased a sliver
of pearlescent seashell
and closed my hand
around this treasure
that I would deliver to you,
my childhood self.

At once I awoke and opened my eyes.
This vision was a gift to me.
This letter is my gift to you.
I enclose this clay and seashell pebble,
and
tell you that it symbolizes
everything that happens.

It is up to you to focus
upon the pearlescent part and
allow the clay to be the carrier
and not distract you.

When looking forward,
focus on what you are wanting,
fixate on the best parts all along.

When looking back
and remembering, you'll find
that you have a string

of pearlescent seashell memories
to count on
and recount
for the rest of your days.
This is the way.

Dory Maguire (she/her) is the author of five self-published collections of poetry, each illustrated with her original photography. Dory's poems have received multiple honorable mentions in the National Federation of State Poetry Societies' annual contests and appear in several anthologies. A committed advocate for poets, Dory hosted her local poetry workshop on her patio during the pandemic when library meetings were suspended, and she remains an active presence in the poetry community, supporting small groups and gatherings both in-person and via Zoom. She lives on a horse farm in Pennsylvania, where she spends her free time sprouting trees, tending forests, and drawing inspiration from the land she stewards.

Letters of Introduction

She will teach you an entirely different way of moving through the world.

-Sara Sobota

...each contributing their own little flavor in the words they teach you.

-Judy Parceaud

Maria Z. Gardner

The lady

A poem for my childhood self

Do you know the lady from the movies in your mind?
The lady who loves you as you are.

Here, you live among landmines.
But there, her calm grounds you.

Look what her love can do.

She's mature. She grows her own lavender.
She tracks celestial movements.
She is a member of an airline loyalty program.

She is cool. She doesn't rush.
Moods don't scare her.
She sits with you through the storm.

She's modern. She says we're all floating dust.
She laughs when you throw your middle fingers in the air.

She doesn't think you're cold.
She screams with you, but never longer than you.
She says fury is information.

She's curious.
She wants to know what you like, and what you don't.
She wants to know things just because.

She is warm.
Her clothes are soft.
She thinks you're funny.
She believes you.

There, you dreamed of her.
But here, you became her.

Look what your love can do.

Hold on to the lady from the movies in your mind.

The lady who loves you as you are.

Maria Z. Gardner (she/her) is a writer and an advocate for survivors of complex trauma. Her work has historically explored the intersections of public policy, research, and the human experience, including writing for the RAND Corporation, the University of Pennsylvania, Drexel University, and more. She believes in telling stories that uplift voices without creating harm.

Judy Parceaud

Letter to a younger me—staying with Auntie Dorothy

Dear Judy,

I was sorry to hear about your mother's accident. I understand that when she was away with your father another car drove into the side of them and the car rolled over. As the roof was open at the time your mother went out that way and landed on her head. This resulted in a fractured skull so she was hospitalized far from home.

You were sent, with your sister Gillian to stay with your godmother, Auntie Dorothy. I don't think you have any idea of the seriousness of this injury but apparently when your mother regained consciousness she was convinced that her three children were in the car with her and had not survived the accident. It was too far away for you all to be taken to visit her so you were asked to write a letter to her to prove that you were still alive. You refused not understanding the seriousness of the situation. So you were placed in the dining room with the curtains closed and told you would stay there until you complied. You wrote the letter but I don't remember how long it took.

Apart from that you loved staying with your aunt and uncle. They took good care of you and as they didn't have any children of their own at the time they were inclined to spoil you. As the middle child with an older brother and a younger sister you weren't used to being special.

That was when your aunt started teaching you to sew. She was a very skilled seamstress. Today I thought to write to you because I found an old thimble. She taught you the importance of using a thimble not just to protect your finger but to be more confident when hand sewing. What she taught you started a life long passion for sewing and even after You married and moved to Canada she continued to encourage you, sending you lovely fabrics to be converted into unique clothes for your children.

But when you stayed with her you would also be spoiled by her mother in law who was like a grandma for you. You never had a grandmother of your own but Auntie Betty (as you called her) didn't have any granddaughters so she used to take you to the ballet and to the opera. You would be dressed in your best finery, your hair beautifully arranged so that your usual sloppy appearance would be transformed. You even wore little white gloves. And then the real fun began, traveling up to London to the Royal Festival Hall to watch a memorable performance with Auntie Betty. You felt really spoilt and proud to be in her company.

Later you would sometimes spend time with Uncle Bob and Auntie Dorothy. The contrast between their orderly life style and the chaos of home with your family was remarkable. Heatherdale, your family's home, was usually cluttered and untidy, the inhabitants often not fully clothed or even naked. The bathroom door was never locked which meant that the family drifted in and out if they needed to use the toilet or brush their teeth, while someone was in the bath. Mealtimes were the only times that you followed your mother's strict protocol. The table had to be set following her guidelines and you all had to change for your evening meal. Sunday lunch was also a special occasion. At Auntie Dorothy's house life was different and very orderly.

Mealtimes were regular, everyone got dressed in the morning and your long hair would be carefully braided and tied up with pretty ribbons.

Auntie Dorothy and Uncle Bob would soon have children of their own, Michael and Peter. By the time Peter was born you were old enough and responsible enough to take him for walks in his pram. How proud you felt walking round to Grannie Elms house showing him off to anyone who cared to look. You would stop along the way to check the butterfly man's garden. He bred and sold butterflies so his trees and bushes had muslin bags tied over their branches. You couldn't see inside the bags but you imagined all kinds of exotic butterflies changing from caterpillars to butterflies inside those bags.

When Queen Elizabeth II was crowned in 1953 your whole family went to stay with Auntie Dorothy and Uncle Bob and joined their neighbours, the Pendowers to watch the event on their television. Not many people had televisions in those days so their living room was filled with friends and neighbours to watch the first coronation to be televised. It was a really festive occasion. Jacques Pendower was a successful writer but as he wrote under as pseudonym we didn't realize how successful he was. Second hand books he wrote still show up on second had book sites and sell for high prices.

As the Gimber boys grew up they would join their next door neighbour John Buck to build canoes. Buck was an orthopaedic surgeon and when his surgery tools were no longer fit for operations they would be recycled and used as woodworking tools for their boat building projects. When Michael went to Cambridge university he continued his love for canoeing and paddled for the university team. Later you will move to Canada and live in the north of Quebec which is a canoer's paradise.

I have never forgotten this happy time of my life and I regret that I couldn't be there to comfort my dear Auntie Dorothy at the end of her life. I visited England when Uncle Bob was an old man, still good humoured and cracking jokes as well as moving his false teeth around just like he did when I was a younger me.

A letter to my younger self, living in France as an "au pair"

Dear Judy.

I know you are living through a major, life changing disappointment but I am confident that you will pick yourself up and continue perhaps in a different, but exciting, direction. The exam you failed has changed your life and dreams. You will not go to medical school but all kinds of other opportunities and adventures are about to unroll.

You know as well as I do that making the most of your life and having a lot of fun brings short lived satisfaction but, not keeping on the path you had pursued for so long, is having a life changing effect on you. Happily all is not lost.

You have already taken a first step to climb out of the ditch of self pity and plan for the next twelve months. You are in France making yourself invaluable to little Philippe. He is almost blind and has several other problems as a result of his seriously premature birth. His parents had hoped to send him to England to a Dr. Bernardo's school for blind children but, at the last minute, they were told that he didn't fit the criteria as he had no sense of space and direction. These are essential qualities if a child is to learn Braille.

I don't remember how you travelled to Bures-sur-Yvette, but now you are settling in with the family. You speak a smattering of school girl French but understanding what other people are saying and figuring out a response is not much short of impossible. Happily the mother is English and the father, as well as their three sons, speak English.

Your first trip driving into Paris was very scary but you are getting more familiar with the gears on the little Citroen deux chevaux (two horsepower). You are managing the speed of the traffic in the city calmly. When somebody rear ended you at a traffic light, the police were called so 6 year old blind Philippe was your interpreter. The police were impressed and amused by the six year old's calm but amused behaviour.

Your dried flower collection, the result of many walks beside the

River Yvette, will remain with you forever as a reminder of your daily walks with Philippe, teaching him to recognize wild flowers not by seeing them but by smelling them. It makes me proud to see you moving ahead to make this rebuilding part of your life so meaningful.

I can tell that the family are helping you learn French, each contributing their own little flavour in the words they teach you. You mention going to the village market with a list (in French), which you had to figure out, making your way through the stalls, ask for what you needed, then pay for with strange French coins and bills. But you managed. I'm so proud of these achievements and remember, through them you are regaining confidence in yourself.

Happily the live-in maid is friendly and cheerful. On days off you sometimes go to the village cinema with her brother and his friend. You ride on the back of their little motorcycles. Sounds a bit dodgy to me!

Philippe has a programme of physiotherapy exercises to do every day. He doesn't always want to do them but I'm sure you will encourage him. In my mind's eyes I can visualize you doing them with him. You told me that you would perhaps pursue your education in that direction. You are beginning to make plans beyond this year in France. I'll share a little secret with you. You so inspired Philippe by making his exercises fun that eventually he qualified to become a physiotherapist himself in spite of being blind.

Christmas will be a test for you as you have never been away from your family at Christmas which, in your family, is very exciting, steeped in family traditions. Your cousins and uncles and aunts gather in your family home with everybody joining in traditional activities. We start with stir Sunday at the end of November. The family joins in to make traditional cakes and puddings which have to be fed with rum or some other liquor until Christmas. Then we would go carol singing, collecting money for the charity of our choice. Christmas Eve would be for setting up the Christmas tree—a group activity. On Christmas morning the children could open the little gifts in their stockings that Santa had dropped off in the night. Then everyone would get dressed for a fancy breakfast and only then did we move into the living room and start opening all the other gifts. As the could be twenty five people in the house it was a lengthy process. Lunch would be a little before three o'clock so we could listen to the King's speech followed by a walk to the river Thames. But this Christmas you will accompany the French family to the mountains for winter sports. Your first experience with snow, sunshine and lots of excitement.

Then on May 1st you will go to a youth hostel and meet a young man who you will fall in love with and eventually marry. You will leave to settle in Canada. But that is another, long story.

So I just wanted to remind you that failing that exam which deprived you of your place in medical school is not the end of the world. Things will change but you will continue on your road to happiness and meet people see places that you can't even imagine. Go for it.

Lots of love from an older you

Judith Clifford Parceaud (she/her) was born on the outskirts of London at the beginning of World War Two. Her family moved to the country when she was seven, where she grew up and lived until she married a Frenchman, leaving England to establish their own family in Canada. She has always enjoyed storytelling and started writing anecdotes about her varied life as a hobby late in life.

Sara Sobota

Dear 22-year-old Sara,

An orange envelope will arrive in the mailbox in October 1990. You will open the orange envelope and take out a Halloween card. A Halloween card?! What even is that? You have never seen one before. You can barely believe someone would take the time to buy a card with you in mind—a person they've never met before. Who thinks like that?

Your mother-in-law does.

Before you travel with your boyfriend Chris to meet his parents the following month, your future mother-in-law asks Chris what you like to eat. She wants to cook food you enjoy. This concept does not exist in your family's home. Everyone eats whatever is put in front of them. This level of attention is crazy, right??

You make the 3-hour drive from your home in the suburbs of Washington, D.C., to Latrobe, Pa. As you approach Chris' hometown, the landscape changes. The only place like it that you've ever been is Grandma Brooker's house, in Marietta, Ohio. As you look out the window at the barns and farmhouses that dot the roads and the wide spaces of open fields in between, passing tractors and hay bales, you feel you're traveling back in time.

Your mother-in-law opens the door with a beaming smile and envelops you in a hug. You can feel the bones along her slender spine, the brush of her carefully styled hair on your cheek. (Years later, you will learn that she goes to the hairdresser every week to have her hair done. She does this until 2025. As long as you know her, she will never once wash her own hair). Your mother-in-law is young—15 years younger than Mom, which will bug Mom in the future. Your boyfriend was the product of a surprise pregnancy when your mother-in-law was 18 years old. You are an immediate insider in the Sobota family, so different from the Brookers, who require a period of distance and social examination before acceptance. Her name is Amber Jeanne, but she goes by Jeanne to everyone except her children. You are instructed to call her Amber.

Over the next few years, you see Amber about every six months. When you do, she not only asks about your job and your family members, but she remembers the details on the next visit. When you and Chris get engaged, she throws an enormous bridal shower at the Latrobe Fire Hall and invites her large family, friends, neighbors, and your mother for a catered lunch. As you and your mother drive to Latrobe, Mom comments on the area's similarity to Marietta, noting, "I forgot how small these houses are." At the shower, you sit in the middle of a banquet table like royalty. People you have never met give you extravagant, handmade presents.

I know you're intrigued reading this, but you're also getting nervous. This kind of instant intimacy makes you suspicious. You're used to Mom, who is sparing with her attention; you've been raised to believe affection must be earned, though you don't realize that yet. You and your siblings believe having less individual attention has made you tougher and more responsible. But Amber's a caretaker. Her job is to keep her own appearance and home clean and orderly and also to make sure everyone has what they like and need—not only when they need it, but even before that.

When you and Chris move to Myrtle Beach in 1993, Amber and Chris' dad, Billy, follow you one year later, buying a house in the next town. This is not as bad as it sounds. You'll have to trust me.

From Amber, you learn how to pay attention to people and surroundings. You become adept at picking out a Christmas gift Amber will like, usually an ensemble from Liz Claiborne or Ruby Road. You learn how to coordinate the look of a room in your house, something Mom either never has time for or cares to do. You also stretch Amber's landscape, introducing her to ideas and ways of seeing the world she hadn't before. You take her to see *Hair*, an art exhibit, a symphony concert—and even, way down the road, a public protest against guns.

You have a baby in January 2000. Mom still lives in Virginia, but with Amber in town, she'll become the grandma your boys know best. Right now, you think that having a grandma nearby would be strange and maybe awful—you've got an aversion to emotional intimacy that you'll recognize in a few years—but believe me, it works. She'll spend time and be close to them in ways you can't imagine right now, because Mom is so proper and stand-offish. You'll learn it's ok to let family members get a little closer.

Though Amber still works full time, she spends every minute of her time off babysitting, which allows you room to breathe. She buys a second-hand crib, a rocking chair, and a baby bathtub so baby Bryce can sleep at her house. As the years pass and your family grows, Amber's help becomes more essential. While you work or run errands, Amber takes the three boys (three boys!) to story time at the library, the movies, the pool, the arcade. She never questions you, criticizes you, or implies anything negative about your mothering. You are immensely grateful for her help and not sure how you would keep your sanity without it.

And yet. You wish she wouldn't take the boys to the movies *every* week and let them buy candy and popcorn. You wish she'd make them clean up their own toys, clear their dishes and put them in the dishwasher (like you've asked her to do) instead of doing it for them. You know, from your own childhood, that doing chores and following routines brings responsibility, not to mention self-reliance you hope your boys will bring with them into adulthood.

In your evolving role as mother, you'll blend the examples you see in Mom and Amber: Set high expectations for the boys but also pay attention to their needs. Know their favorite meals, listen to their problems, and have warm socks and sweatshirts in their dressers before they ask for them.

You'll also learn that being a lifelong caregiver has costs. When Amber's birthday comes around, nobody in the family knows what she likes because she's always worried about everyone else. In contrast, you want to be a mother whose kids know what you like to read, listen to, watch, eat. You want them to know what you believe and why, what is important to you and how you understand yourself in the world. As the years pass, you wish more and more that Amber had had the opportunity to figure that out for herself.

Right now, you've never even imagined your mother-in-law or what kind of mother you'll be. And you shouldn't—there's plenty of time for that. But know that your mother-in-law will be a central figure in your life. She will teach you an entirely different way of moving through the world, and she will leave an indelible mark on your children. You're lucky, Sara. You will be a warmer mother and better person for knowing Amber.

Love,
Sara

Sara Sobota (she/her) is a writer and educator based in Myrtle Beach, S.C. She teaches and writes at Coastal Carolina University as principal lecturer of English and editor/lead writer of Tapestry, the alumni magazine of the Edwards College of Humanities and Fine Arts. Sara holds an M.F.A. in nonfiction from the Bennington Writing Seminars. She serves as nonfiction editor at The Petigru Review, the literary journal of the South Carolina Writers Association, and is working on a memoir about the first year of her son's recovery from alcohol addiction.

Melissa Whiteford St. Clair

Dear Newlywed Military Spouse Me,

You've just said "I do" to your high school sweetheart, a newly commissioned Second Lieutenant in the United States Marine Corps. You do not know what you've gotten yourself into. Soon you'll hear someone say, "If the military wanted you to have a wife, they would have issued one." But don't be discouraged.

I'm going to borrow another line of military speak: BLUF. That's Bottom Line Up Front. And this is what you will need to remember: YOU HAVE NOT GONE MIA. YOU ARE STILL YOU.

Because anyone affiliated with the military loves a good checklist, I will share my top five insights before I share a poem about a conversation in the green room on your wedding day.

Ready to copy? Here goes:

- You will learn military training and workup cycles can be more difficult than deployments.
- You will discover a portable career through entrepreneurship and remain an advocate for military spouse employment.
- You will meet friends who become family.
- You will be bestowed a godsend gift of poetry as a processing mechanism while studying racial equity and civil rights. Yes, poetry unexpectedly surfaced to answer questions on the quest for knowledge about the African American experience in the United States, fueled by Harriet Tubman's heroic flight to freedom.
- You find your voice after feeling as though you've been on mute.

Here's that poem I mentioned:

Clinging Vine

Penny in her shoe
Something borrowed, something blue.

Heart a-flutter in the ready room
About to walk down the aisle to wed her groom.

The advice received as she envisioned hearts entwined,
"No man wants a clinging vine..."

Heartsink for that split second of time.
Tucked away to the back of her mind
As the organ played and the wedding bells chimed.

Little did the soothsayer know
As the spouse of an active-duty Marine
She would live her life predominantly solo
While her grunt answered the call of the DOD's machine.

A demanding gun club that claimed his attention
Moving from duty station to duty station triggered constant
reinvention.

Trailing him. She lost herself; she found herself and lost herself
again.
Being hyper-aware of the boxes a military spouse finds
oneself put in.

While he climbed the ranks
She clung to planting roots.

Bloom where you're planted,
A quote for living the military spouse lifestyle often used.

Many a holiday, anniversary, birthday spent alone
Waiting for mail or a call from an overseas sat phone.

The September birthday flower, a morning glory
The flowers are resilient with the ability to grow through
adversity.
Traits to help her meander through her journey.

Vines coil, twist, and bend
Making concessions
Altering directions
Weaving a circle of support, a network of friends.

Just being yourself was finally a truth she realized near his career's end.

About 1% of the U.S. population currently serves in the military. Welcome to the 1% club. Semper Fidelis!

Retiree Military Spouse Me

Melissa Whiteford St. Clair (she/her), founder of White Girl Advocacy, is a poet and social justice advocate. She shares her message of unity and creativity through interactive workshops, poetry readings, and community events. Melissa has published two books of poetry and a self-guided workbook. She is a contributing poet to the "South Carolina Bards Poetry Anthology" and "Finding Common Ground Leaning in to Listen." Her poem "Harriet's Feat to Freedom" was featured on the Hilton Head Island Poetry Trail at Mitchelville. She was honored to be part of the Piccolo Spoleto Sundown Poetry Series in 2025.

Heather Branham

Follow Your Light Home: A Letter to Me at Age 4

Dear Heather,

I know you're confused right now because the grownups are making grownup decisions that don't make sense. You thought everyone in your family would always be together. When you found out that your grandparents were moving away, that they wouldn't live in the same house—or even the same town—as you, your whole world collapsed. You thought they were your home. *If they're gone, where is home*? I know this is scary, and it's not your fault. You didn't do anything wrong.

In a few years, when people start asking what you want to be when you grow up, you'll say that you want to write children's books. People will think that's cute and funny. By the time you're grown up and have had many jobs that have nothing to do with writing children's books, you'll start to wonder how this answer made any sense. Then one day while you're sitting on the beach, listening for a healing message from the ocean, a story will flow out of you with such ease that you'll realize that it had been inside you for years, waiting for the right moment to be told. I wrote this story for you. We wrote this story together. This is our story.[1]

> This is the story of a baby sea turtle hatchling named Flippy. When sea turtle mamas lay their eggs, they leave as soon as the eggs are covered by the sand, weeks before the baby sea

---

1 This story was inspired by my visit to the Karen Beasley Sea Turtle Rescue and Rehabilitation Center in Surf City, North Carolina. When my tour of the facility reached the room housing the recovering sea turtles, I found myself in a large room filled with several tanks of water (picture a really big kiddie pool made of heavy duty plastic), each containing one or two sick or injured sea turtles who had been rescued and rehabilitated and were waiting to be released. What I didn't notice at first was that all the sea turtles were facing the same direction. The tour guide explained that sea turtles have an "internal GPS" that points them in the direction of the ocean. This windowless room was at least a mile from the beach, but these sea turtles still knew where to find their home. I also learned that when sea turtles hatch, they rely on the moon to guide them to the ocean. The moonlight from above reflects off the surface of the water, and the baby sea turtles follow this light home.

turtles even hatch. Flippy was one of those babies, on her own from day one. Even so, Flippy grew and grew until one day she outgrew that shell and hatched. Out of her shell, Flippy was confused. *Where was her mother? How would she get home? Where was home?* It had been so cozy and warm in her shell, but now Flippy felt small, unprotected and so scared.

She also felt a little cramped. She had to get out of this nest. Scared as she was, Flippy stretched and pushed against her hatching siblings. As she did, she felt something deep inside pulling her toward the light above their nest in the sand. There was a pulsing in her chest, like her heart wanted to expand all the way outside her body and touch that light. She wasn't sure why she felt this way or where it would take her, but Flippy knew in her little sea turtle body that that light had something she needed. She just had to reach it.

When she finally made it out of the nest, Flippy realized that her work had just begun. Getting out of the nest was the easy part. Now she had to flipper her way through the sand toward the light, which seemed to be not only above her, but also in front of her. Flippy was focused and determined. Her knowing grew with every inch she moved forward toward that big, bright, beautiful light: that light held her future. That light would lead her home.

The moment Flippy's little body touched the salty water of the ocean, she knew this was where she belonged, where she was meant to be. She knew because the light from above that had pulled her up and out of the nest, the light before her that had coaxed her across the sandy beach, was radiated through her entire body, filling every cell. She relaxed and let the ocean current carry her for a while, resting after all that hard work.

Flippy was proud of herself for making it out of the nest and into the ocean, but she also felt sad because she was still scared. *Where would she sleep? What would she eat? How would she survive in the vast ocean all by herself?* Flippy's heart broke, spilling light into the water all around her. She flipped and flopped, struggling to stay afloat, wondering if she should try to swim back to the beach. Then something miraculous happened. As Flippy flapped and flailed, she bumped into something solid. It was another sea turtle! And this sea turtle was shining light from their broken heart too. When they looked at each other and smiled, both of their lights grew brighter.

Flippy had been so focused on finding home that she'd forgotten that she was surrounded by other little sea turtle bodies. All around her the surface of the water sparkled with their brilliance. They felt just as scared and confused as she did, and they had followed their lights into the ocean too—an instinct they inherited from their sea turtle ancestors. As she looked around, Flippy realized that she had never been alone. Her fear had kept her from seeing what was just within reach all along. And in that moment, Flippy knew she had everything she would ever need. This must be home.

You, little one, are like that baby sea turtle searching for home. You may be scared and confused, but you also have a light in you that guides you to the people and places that you need to feel at home. Whenever you feel like home is far away, when you believe you've got to do it all alone, when the waves get choppy and your broken heart is being tossed about, leaking its light into the sea, remember to look up. Reach out. Be still and notice what you feel inside, where your heart is pulling you next. That's how you'll find the light that leads you home. You just have to trust it and let it lead the way.

Love,

Heather

Heather Branham (she/her) was born near the ocean and followed her light home to the mountains of western North Carolina, where she spends her time studying and sharing healing practices rooted in relationship. Connect with her at SeventhHouseHealing.com.

Letters of Instruction

* *Take typing instead of shorthand. You're going to need to use something called a "keyboard" soon.*

  -Mare Schumacher

* *Always carry hand lotion in the winter and bug spray in the summer. You won't regret it!*

  -Heather Branham

* *Take your Spanish language classes more seriously. And don't let Kristin get a tattoo in Mexico.*

  -Lynn Lipinksi

* *Do not cut off all your hair. You are not Meg Ryan or Halle Berry.*

  -Patricia Hatch

* *Eat more chocolate.*

  -Charlie Hebert-Russell

* *Never say no to more books.*

  -V. Rendina

Ed McCall

Dear Eddie,

You don't know me, but I know you. I am you. Or was. So much you need to know. Some you won't believe. Some of it you will probably ignore.

First: Study a little harder. Stop sitting in the back of the class trying to hide from the teacher because you didn't do your homework. Do the damned homework. Read the assignments. Really. It is that easy. Make an effort.

Second: College is not Big High School! It is different. Sit at the front of the class. Ask questions. Don't talk over the professor. Take notes, study for the exams, and don't be a smart ass. Do the damned homework.

Third: In your Senior year of high school, you will be offered a slot at South Carolina Boys State. Take it. It will be better for your spirit than a week at the beach.

Fourth: Travel. Lots. Memories last longer than things. Wake to new horizons. Explore other countries. Learn other languages (yes, you can do it). Money returns. Time does not.

Fifth: The house on Kathryn Street in Cary, North Carolina, will feel like home the moment you enter the front door. Never sell that house. It holds a piece of your soul.

Last: Deaths of family members will be hard. Cry at the funerals. Laugh too. Deaths of your pets will be as hard. Cry when you bury them in your backyard. You will mourn the death of your first dog for your whole life. That's OK. Jeep will be standing with your Mom and Dad, waiting for you when you die, too.

Live your life well. Love ferociously. Laugh lots. Enjoy every birthday you have.

Love,
Me. You. Us.

Ed McCall (he/him) has been retired for many years from work in insurance and software, but is still working. Now in retail. He considers himself to be a writer, still learning the craft. He can be found exploring new places, traveling, and enjoying coffee shops everywhere. He lives in Irmo, SC.

Sybil St. Claire

A Letter to My Younger Selves: Notes on Growing Brave, Blooming Messy & Staying Juicy

Dear Sprout,

You were not planted with intention—just a seed scattered by chance. Not chosen. Not hoped for. You were replanted many times. Moved again and again. Lifted from soft soil, set down in stone. And still, you grew. You always grew. Endurance is not the same as being nurtured, but sometimes survival is the only kind of growth we're allowed. Talk to the trees, the sky, the wild ones. They will always listen.

When you were quite young, you learned that silence has a cost. One night, a puppy cried and no one came—you learned not every gardener cares for the vulnerable. When you found its small body cold by morning, something in you vowed, I will be the one who cares. Keep that vow. That was not a wound; it was the first bloom of your fierce compassion. It was the moment you began to carry the medicine. When those boys and men violated you, that was their rot, not your ruin. You did not invite the damage; you survived it. Burn what you need to and plant marigolds over the ashes if you must. You owe your healing to no one's sense of propriety.

To the woman who weathered her twenties, reinvented in her thirties, unraveled in her forties, and still dared to hope in her fifties—you all kept blooming (and occasionally combusting). You will often prune with dull shears, but what a riot of color the garden will be. You will found a theatre, become a professor, marry and divorce, water hope and watch it wilt, plant yourself on ships and teach on floating gardens. You'll live off the grid and dance in the dust of Burning Man. You'll run away to Italy, because joy sometimes speaks with an accent, and you'll have more than one wildfire romance that jolts you back to life and singes your eyebrows off. You will fall in love with impossible people, not because you are foolish, but because you are a seed that keeps believing in spring. Love will always be your way of photosynthesizing the impossible. And you will learn—some people are seasons, some are compost, and some are perennials.

Some days, love will look like fur in your breakfast and a tiny creature claiming you as home. You will teach, planting seeds of courage until one day an entire forest emerges. You will grow a colorful bouquet of friends—loud ones who make you pee-laugh, soft ones who arrive with soup and sanctuary, feral ones who drag you dancing under the moon, and steady ones who hold a mirror to your magic. Sometimes your chosen family will be the whole damn garden!

You will dance like a flower on espresso—in drum circles, in your kitchen while dinner burns, in countries where you don't speak the language, but your hips do. Shake out the grief before it calcifies. Nature will keep saving you—kayaking on quiet rivers, riding horses on the beach, lying on the grass watching clouds suggest risqué shapes. The earth will be your therapist. She charges in dirt under your fingernails.

To the woman who stays hidden for far too long, frightened and aching, it's okay. Some seeds stay dormant until the fire. When you are ready, a quiet urge will call you upward. The sun will not scold you for how long you hid. To the one losing teeth, hair, and health—this too is a season. Compost what you must. Sickness, fear, fatigue, all of it can be turned under. The earth knows how to recycle pain and loss into transformation and growth. You will create a sprawling perennial meant to help others grow their own gardens. You will build a legacy that outlives heartbreak. Sometimes survival turns into service.

Know that retirement will not feel like the end—it will feel like the harvest. Students will still reach out with stories of how you helped them bloom. You will not be fading, you will be ripening. Stay juicy! And to the one who still tries to grow love in hard soil, stop watering what you do not wish to grow, my love. You are not a gardener of suffering. You are a cultivator of wonder. You carry the medicine. There is still time for gentler blooms.

Yes, the soil will be rough, but oh, the parts drenched in sunlight and enriched with love: questionable decisions made under starlight, a heart swollen with too much feeling to fit neatly anywhere, forest bathing and skinny-dipping, mother nature calling you tenderly home. All glimpses of the lush garden still ahead of you. Hang on—there are wild blooms emerging everywhere!

And in the end? There will be laughter. Loud, real, snort-laughter. There will be nights you feel held by the universe. Mornings where your hot chocolate tastes like hope. Animals who believe in your greatness. Friends who refuse to let you wither. There will be love that never ends and love that does—and all of it will teach you.

With muddy hands, silver hair, and laugh lines etched by dark and light, I'm here to say, keep going. It's ridiculously worth it.

~ The Woman You Keep Growing Into

Gardening Tips for Future You
(Who Will Absolutely Forget and Need Reminding)

- Not every seed will be—some bloom briefly or not at all, some blow away, and that's not failure, that's life.
- If a garden keeps draining you dry, it's not a garden, it's a desert in floral cosplay. Leave before you become dust.
- Fertilizer often smells awful at first, healing can too. Give it time before deciding it's just crap.
- If you wouldn't water it in real life, stop watering it emotionally. You know who and what I'm talking about.
- You don't have to bloom constantly. Some seasons exist only to let your roots rest.
- Dance like a dandelion in a storm—flexible, ridiculous, wild—and still standing when the sky clears.
- If it brings laughter, goosebumps, or wonder—that's sunlight. Tilt toward it without apology.
- Some people are shade. Grow there only if the shade feels like shelter, not deprivation.
- Define what "weed" means to you. Pull them early, resentment grows faster than joy.
- Never apologize for being a wildly overgrown, technicolor, joy-making jungle of becoming. Lawns are for people afraid of surprise.

Sybil St. Claire, M.F.A., (she/her) is a Senior Lecturer Emerita of Theatre, a Creative Wellbeing Consultant, and an expressive arts facilitator. She is the Founding Director of The Creative Wellbeing Institute and author of Creative Wellbeing: An Expressive Arts Journey into the Heart of Human Flourishing. *Her work is grounded in the belief that creativity is an innate human capacity that, when engaged, strengthens resilience, supports emotional regulation, and enriches wellbeing.*

Linda M. Crate

lessons for my younger self:

crying doesn't make you weak:
only human,
people are rarely pleased and
can be extremely fickle
so it's okay to choose and be
your authentic self,
there's nothing wrong with
being different
and being weird is actually a
compliment,
don't change yourself to fit in
because it will only make
you sad,
people will treat you like
how they value you
no matter how much love
you pour into them
so make sure you love and
honor yourself more,
your magic and the mythology of your
bones is beautiful and worthy
no matter what,
you are of value even if you're fat,
being skinny doesn't need
to be a life goal but being healthy
should be,
don't starve yourself just because
they try to shame you
for eating every body needs fuel
and every body is good
even yours,
doing your best looks different
every day,

your fire and your rebellion to
stay yourself is worth it,
it's better to be lonely than to
have a friend who doesn't
value you or respect you,
take more risks because
sometimes you are rewarded
for taking a chance at
something new,
do more of what makes you happy,
stop worrying so much
about everything,
don't wait so much just go
and do it,
life is beautiful and long
but goes by fast so
enjoy more of it,
not everyone will hurt you
it's okay to open up your heart,
when people show their true
colors believe them,
you can't save anyone
that doesn't want to be
saved or change anyone
who doesn't want to change,
you can walk a path that is different
from everyone else's
life is a journey not a race;
eat the ice cream,
dance in the rain,
pet more dogs,
spontaneous adventures
can be fun,
there's good in every day
even the bad and heavy
ones,
you are more loved than you
sometimes feel,
i love you.

Linda M. Crate (she/her) is a Pennsylvanian writer whose poetry, short stories, articles, and reviews have been published in a myriad of magazines, both online and in print. She has seventeen published chapbooks, the latest being: only the future knows (Alien Buddha Press, November 2025).

Lynn Lipinski

THE DANGEROUS ART OF NEEDING NOTHING

Dear Nine-Year-Old Me,

Next year at Cheryl's house in Fayetteville, you'll be having a sleepover when her family's tabby cat jumps onto your sleeping bag sometime after midnight. You love animals, so you'll pet his soft fur in the dark, not knowing that within minutes your eyes will start watering, then burning and swelling.

You'll lie there in Cheryl's bedroom, listening to her steady breathing, as your nose becomes stuffy and your chest grows tight. The house is dark and quiet. Everyone is asleep. Your throat starts to feel scratchy, then raw, like you've swallowed sandpaper. Each breath becomes work—shallow and insufficient, like trying to breathe through a straw.

In the darkness, you'll run through your familiar calculations: If I wake someone up, I'll ruin the sleepover. If they call Mom at 2 AM, she'll be furious, not just about being woken up but about me being "dramatic" and "attention-seeking." Better to handle this alone, like always. So you'll stay still in your sleeping bag, eyes streaming, chest tight, trying to breathe quietly while everyone sleeps around you.

But here's what I want you to know: that ten-year-old logic is wrong. When you can't breathe properly, when your face is swelling and your throat feels raw, that's exactly when you need to wake up Cheryl's mom. Shake her shoulder gently. Say these exact words: "I think I'm allergic to your cat. Can you help me?"

Your need for air isn't going to ruin anything. Your breathing matters more than anyone's sleep. Practice saying it now: "Can you help me?" Those aren't dangerous words. They're the words that choose your needs over your fear.

I know you're living with Mom's whiplash moods—chocolate chip cookies and smiles at 3 PM, screaming fits by dinner. But the survival skill of self-reliance you're perfecting is becoming a trap. That allergy attack at Cheryl's house is just one example of how only relying on yourself is a dangerous habit.

This same calculation—acting like you need nothing from no one—will follow you everywhere. You'll skip study groups when algebra becomes abstract puzzles you can't solve. You'll sit alone in calculus, pretending to understand. Again and again, you'll choose the familiar ache of isolation over the risk of admitting you need help. You'll become the friend everyone turns to for support, but you'll never learn how to let them return the favor.

I know what you're thinking. You don't know who to ask for help about coping with your mother's alcohol-fueled outbursts. Before your older sister left for college, she used to rush you out of the house the moment Mom started dropping ice cubes in her lowball glass at noon on Saturday. Your sister would drive you to the record store or the mall, anywhere so you wouldn't be underfoot for whatever came next.

The terrible day Mom punched her hand through the glass of the post lantern in the front yard, your sister carried you back in the house so you wouldn't see the blood streaming down her arm, wouldn't see the glass shard in her hand as she threatened to slit her wrist right there in front of anyone passing by. I know you still saw enough to be terrified. I know that without your sister's protection, you're scared to be in the house alone with Mom.

First, I want you to know that in a few months, something will shift. Mom will stop drinking and start going to meetings where she learns how to stay sober. She'll get busy with college classes and a job at the drugstore and fighting to stop them from building a nuclear power plant in our backyard. She'll start picking you up from school again. She'll ask about your day and actually listen to your answer. She'll read you stories before bed without her words slurring together. The mom you glimpse sometimes between the rages? You're going to see her more and more. In the meantime, your sister is still there for you, she's just further away. Call her or write her a letter; she will listen.

I know asking for help has backfired before. Like the day you ran barefoot to the neighbor's house when Mom dumped all your dresser drawers onto the floor because you lost a gold belt, desperate for somewhere safe to wait it out. The neighbor walked you home with kind intentions, and Mom thanked her with that bright, false smile before closing the door and slapping you hard across the face.

You weren't wrong to ask for help. You were wrong about who Mom was really angry at—not you, but the world that might see her secret. That neighbor didn't know what else to do. And that humiliating moment? It might be exactly what pushes Mom to finally get sober.

Your dad doesn't know what to do about Mom's rages either, but he loves you and he will listen. The ice clinking in Mom's glass is a dreadful sound, but equally dreadful is Dad scraping his car keys from the kitchen table, the front door closing behind him as he leaves you there to pick up the pieces of whatever her rage broke that day. He's not fleeing because he thinks you're to blame or that you can fix it somehow. Dad can rebuild a jet engine with his bare hands, but he has no tools for Mom's rage. So when the yelling starts, he just walks away.

Find him on a quiet Saturday afternoon when he's under the hood of the Oldsmobile, old sitcoms crackling from the small TV perched on his workbench—Ralph Kramden's bluster mixing with the smell of motor oil and WD-40. Sit on the rolling creeper he uses to slide under "Yellowbird" and breathe in that particular combination of grease and Old Spice that means safety to you.

Tell him how your stomach knots when you hear his keys scraping across the kitchen table. Tell him you don't understand why Mom's anger can turn so sharp, so fast. Ask him why he leaves you alone with her when the drinking starts.

He'll probably set down his wrench and look at you with those tired but kind brown eyes. He might not have answers—I think he'll tell you he doesn't understand it either. But he'll pull you close with his oil-stained hands and tell you how proud he is of you, how much he loves you. Sometimes just knowing you're not alone in the confusion makes all the difference.

You need to know this is really Mom's problem to solve. She loves you just as much as Dad does. Mom's anger isn't about you—it's about pain she's been carrying since she was your age. That doesn't make it okay, but it makes it not your fault.

So hang in there and don't think you are to blame for these things. You are not responsible for fixing the adults around you.

But you are responsible for learning that asking for help is not weakness. It is taking control of your life. It's unlearning the lesson that your needs are dangerous, that your voice doesn't matter, that love comes with conditions you can never quite meet.

Start small. When you're confused in math class, raise your hand. When you're sad about missing your sister, tell Dad. When you can't breathe, speak up. Each time you ask for help, you're saying your life matters. You're saying you deserve to breathe freely, to understand math, to feel safe in your own house.

Here's the thing about courage: it's not the absence of fear. It's speaking up when your throat is closing and everyone else is asleep. It's knocking on Dad's garage door when your hands are shaking. It's believing that your need for air, for understanding, for safety, matters as much as anyone else's comfort.

The little girl who will lie silent in that sleeping bag, struggling to breathe? She's braver than she knows. But the woman writing this letter learned something that girl couldn't see yet: the bravest thing you can do is let someone else care about whether you're okay.

So when you can't breathe at Cheryl's house—and you will remember this letter in that dark moment—whisper her name. Reach out your hand. Ask for help. Not because you're weak, but because you're finally strong enough to believe you matter.

That's the real dangerous art, Nine-Year-Old Me: learning that needing nothing from no one isn't strength. Learning to need—and be needed—is where the real living begins.

Lynn Lipinski (she/her) holds an M.F.A. degree from Mount St. Mary's University. Her professional writing has been featured in the Los Angeles Times, UCLA Magazine, Trojan Family Magazine, as well as multiple literary publications such as Woven Tale Review, Red Earth Review, and Conclave. In 2021, she received the Rilla Askew Prize for Short Fiction from Balkan Press.

Michelle Elisburg

Dear (Younger) Michelle,

Don't worry that you never managed to have a nickname. I've tried as an adult, and it never caught on. But at least most people stopped singing, "Michelle, My Belle..." so that's something to be thankful for. This is my message for you: live with more gratitude.

That song you sing at Jewish camp and Hebrew school is not just a catchy tune, but an intention for the day: to thank God for waking up to a new day.

> Modeh ani l'fanecha
> *I give thanks before you,*
>
> Melech Chai V'kayam
> *Living and Eternal Ruler*
>
> Shehechezarta bi nishmati b'chemla,
> *that you have returned within me my soul with compassion.*
>
> rabah emunatecha.
> *(how) abundant is Your faithfulness*

מוֹדֶה אֲנִי לְפָנֶיךָ מֶלֶךְ חַי וְקַיָּם, שֶׁהֶחֱזַרְתָּ בִּי נִשְׁמָתִי בְּחֶמְלָה. רַבָּה אֱמוּנָתֶךָ

It doesn't matter what we did yesterday or last night; nothing can taint those first innocent words that sit at our primal consciousness. Our soul is returned to us, and anything is possible.

Treasure your high school trip to Israel in 1987 when you are able to sit on a hill on the border of Gaza looking at a simple checkpoint. All of that will change over time. By my age there will be a terrible attack on October 7, 2023, against the Israeli border towns by Hamas terrorists from Gaza. They will massacre over 1200 Israelis and take 254 people hostage.

Some of those hostages will describe how they would say this prayer every morning, grateful for a gasp of stale air and a morsel of food. Others will describe how they kept Shabbat, even in an airless tunnel in darkness. Somehow they knew. Do these prayers with intention and always do something for Shabbat. It will nourish you in ways you can't imagine.

Always write thank you cards. Mom and Dad will make you do this, and it really is a significant routine I learned and passed on to my children. Express gratitude for someone thinking of you. It is always meaningful to receive a thank you note.

You will pay attention to those who don't send one. It's such a small thing but has very big meaning.

I didn't realize how important the thank you letter was to Mom and Dad until their 50th anniversary was coming up. Mom gave me a letter she found that she had written to Grandma Bert and Grandpa Mack thanking them for hosting their wedding. From Acapulco on their honeymoon! I feel like there were more fun things to do, but if it was that important to show gratitude that you'd write a letter to your parents on your honeymoon, then it must be important and worthwhile.

Our intended gift was to write them thank you letters for what they have taught and given our family. The others managed to do this on time. It's taken me 10 years, but they will receive the letter in this book by their 60th anniversary, demonstrating that it is never too late to show gratitude.

Try to write a real letter on real paper and send with a real stamp from the post office. Resist the temptation to only send texts or emails. These are fleeting and will disappear, but the paper note will appear years later and give you joy when you don't even know you need it.

That is my wish for you.
Michelle

Michelle Elisburg (she/her) is a pediatrician in a Federally Qualified Health Center in Louisville, KY, where she talks with versions of her younger self on a daily basis. A native of Potomac, MD, she now lives in southern Indiana, across the river from Louisville.

Dr. Elisburg believes in the power of storytelling in all forms and writes essays as well as creates scrapbooks to express both the written word and visual images. She has been married for 26 years, has a grumpy old man rescue dog and two young adult daughters who write thoughtful thank you notes.

Catherine Parceaud

Letter to My Newly Diagnosed Self

Dear Catherine,

A CT scan has revealed an opacity on your top right lung and you're a mess. I know, it's a total shocker not to mention you haven't smoked in over 25 years. You have no symptoms, you're feeling great. You are shocked, beyond shocked. The anomaly was discovered while investigating something unrelated which means it's an incidental finding.

Incidental finding sounds so innocent; almost playful. It will lead to a lengthy, frightening investigation period; your agenda filling up with multiple appointments for scans, blood tests, bronchoscopy, biopsy, breathing capacity tests and more.

No wonder you're feeling perilously untethered and lost; this is a life changing event.

It's tough, it's real tough to have a suspicious-looking nodule on your lung. You're freaking out and it's ok to feel that way.

During this period, despair inhabits your mind and dark thoughts bounce around like a pinball with no escape. You have always considered lung cancer as an excruciating death sentence. Fear and disbelief hold you captive as you sit through test after test, spending hours in different waiting rooms. You saw your father die from lung cancer and the images are vivid in your mind. You're hurt, confused, terrified, incapable of focusing on anything. Death is palpable all the time now. Nothing will ever be like it was before. You feel that your life is done. You'll never feel joy again. You feel dead already. You're so lonely.

It's a whirl. A whirl of destruction, pieces of you flying off in all directions, spinning back towards you and away again.

I want you to hold on, Catherine. Just hold on. Although it seems impossible now, calmer waters will return.

Two years after the initial CT scan set the storm in motion, I'm here to let you know that yes, your life will change forever. The lung cancer diagnosis is confirmed but your outlook will shift, and release you from that dark, hopeless cave. The chaotic state you're experiencing is not sustainable. You can't be in panic mode for the rest of your life, however long that turns out to be. I can tell you that after surgery to remove the tumour along with the upper right lobe of your lung, you will learn to carry on.

You've always felt wonder at the beauty of the natural world, but it's amplified now and it puts things into perspective. Walking helps you notice the splendour of nature and has the added benefit of grounding. Poetry and books about nature are another source of spiritual nourishment. You'll become more level-headed and philosophical about your situation. Thankfully, the period of shock, doom and paralysis will play itself out. I'm not saying it's nirvana—low periods will cycle back but it's nothing like before. You will feel joy again and it turns out you have reserves of tremendous strength.

You discover that you can't expect people to fully understand and support you. The more you crave support, the more you'll be disappointed. Stop focusing on what others don't understand, they haven't traveled your road. Just concentrate on your serenity and bring energy back around to yourself. What will be, will be. Nurture yourself, practice self compassion; you will be a better, happier person for it. Cherish the special light that glows within you, nurture and keep it lit. Flourishing is fun!

I want you to know that the suffering and resilience of people will resonate with you on a deeper level. You'll feel a deep sense of kinship with other survivors and those who have passed. For you, like them, there are no guarantees of what lies ahead. But their strength, like ripples on water, disperse and reach your shores. Yes, one day you'll die of something, and it may well be cancer. But in the meantime, you'll live.

I love you, Catherine. I wish this wasn't happening but that won't get us anywhere. We need to embrace destiny and move forward with gratitude for the gifts that lie ahead. Because no matter what, there are always gifts along the way.

Take care.

With lots of love,

Catherine xoxoxoxoxox

Catherine Parceaud (she/her) lives in both the Lower Saint Lawrence region of Quebec and Nunavik. She is a recently retired college teacher and lung cancer survivor. The newfound freedom allows her to practice much-loved activities like walking daily in wild areas, reading, writing, sewing, and learning about all kinds of new stuff. She loves spending time outdoors with her naturalist husband, exploring, birdwatching, and fly fishing.

Susan Michele Coronel

Fall for the girl you already are.

Dear Self at 17,

You've always been enough, though you never knew it.

Don't be like Celery, the stuffed rabbit with the sewn-shut mouth. You are a monostitch—a startling fragment with its own integrity.

Your body is your own: wide hips, curly hair whispering heft. No need to hide beneath the pageboy pink wig or Elvira hairpiece with its black spikes. In time the burgundy Manic Panic on your tips will fade, and you'll return to your original mousy loam.

Lean into the cavern of your back like a cello, its resonance vibrating from your throat down to your Doc Martens. Defeats will eat at you, but not kill you. If you love yourself more than anything, you'll never lack love.

When you scribbled notes on discarded *New York Times* pages on the Long Island Railroad, would you have guessed a few commuters would actually read them? You gave them hope when they thought their future ended at the edge of their briefcases.

And not only them. Some of your pen pals kept the letters you sent—rambling passages, with the longing to connect through words outside the confines of space and time.

You can fit so much more into your pockets, and I urge you to share more of your words without censorship. Your words matter—resting somewhere between charm and courage.

I won't reveal how your life will unfold; discovery is yours. But if I can influence your future in any positive way, I gladly will. A few requests:

1. Interview Grandpa before it's too late.

His physical heart will weaken, though his emotional heart places you at its center. One day, standing ankle-deep in the 21st century, you'll be grateful you recorded the stories of a boy who survived the Russian Revolution. You'll kiss the ground again and again, remembering you're alive because Grandpa hid in barns and churches after his father died—until his mother's search party from Poland found him.

2. Know that Grandma won't live forever.

Her strength, humor, and warm recipes suggest she might, but she won't. One day, leaning over the kitchen sink as she washes dishes, she'll tell you, *Sometimes we just have to face facts. I'm not going to be around much longer*. She'll urge you to take the family photo albums, knowing how deeply you treasure them and that you'll be their best guardian. You'll say, *Grandma, don't say such things,* and leave them on the bottom shelf, believing she can outlast time.

Take them, with love. Seal them in boxes. Keep them safe. One day, you'll pass them to your children and grandchildren.

3. You don't need a boyfriend to feel complete.

Savor your trips abroad, late-night concerts at The Ritz and Danceteria, sparkly dresses and black eyeliner. The freedom to move and discover is what makes adolescence vibrant. Enjoy the beautiful people you meet and the dreams they spark, but don't force coupling.

If you take these actions now, your life will be salted with treasures instead of regrets. Otherwise, it will feel like an apricot stone lodged in your shoe, impossible to shake loose.

To be drenched with love, you must get wet. To linger and not act is to suffer.

Embrace what's yours; it belongs to you alone. There will be less to grapple with if you engage deeply with life now, listening more intently to its quiet, persistent melody.

Your Loving Future Self

Susan Michele Coronel's debut collection, "In the Needle, A Woman" (Finishing Line Press, 2025) won the 2024 Donna Wolf Palacio Poetry Prize. Three of the poems in the collection were nominated for the Pushcart Prize. Her poems have appeared in numerous journals including MOM Egg Review, One Art, Pedestal, and SWWIM. In 2023, she won the Massachusetts Poetry Festival's First Poem Award. She lives in Ridgewood, Queens.

Letters of Witness to the Past

I remember you...
...Let me imagine you then...
-Candice Daquin

I remember you.
-Dahlia Fisher

...Just like your tongue can find
the sore spot of a cavity
even after it's been carefully filled...
-Sarah Josephine Pennington

Tisha Marie Fritz

Dear Eighteen-Year-Old Me,

You're doing everything you can to stay afloat, and no one sees it. The choir rehearsals, the clubs, the church, the laughter with friends, the late nights with John, every single thing you can fit into a day. You fill every hour without even knowing why, only that stillness feels dangerous. The ambition is real, but it has no direction yet, just a restless energy driving you from one thing to the next. You keep moving, thinking the noise might somehow quiet the ache you can't yet name.

I want to tell you something: you're not broken for needing the noise. You're trying to survive feelings you don't yet have words for. One day, you'll learn that exhaustion can be a form of self-protection, that depression isn't laziness or weakness, it's your mind saying please slow down and listen.

There's something else I need to tell you about your little brother. He's still the boy who adores you, even when it doesn't look like it. I know you're already moving fast toward a future that will pull you in every direction. But don't let him slip through the cracks of your ambition. Write him notes. Sit on the edge of his bed sometimes, even when you're tired. Tell him you love him out loud. The years will pass faster than you think, and silence will cost you more than words ever could.

When you fight later, don't let pride win. Don't let paperwork and pain draw a line you never cross again. Keep reaching for him. One day, you'll lose him at thirty-three, and that loss will rearrange your soul. You'll carry both love and regret in the same hand.

But his life will leave you with a truth you'll never forget. Every birthday is a blessing. Aging isn't something to dread; it's a privilege. When you turn forty, you'll whisper *thank you* instead of *how did I get here*. You'll see your gray hairs as proof of survival, your laugh lines as evidence of grace. You'll love the woman you become because you finally stopped running from her.

Keep your heart open, even when it hurts. Keep your feet grounded, even when you want to flee. Love people in real time. And remember, you are already enough—wise, radiant, and whole, even in your confusion.

With love,
The You Who Finally Stayed

Tisha Marie Fritz is a writer and storyteller whose work explores healing, motherhood, faith, resilience, and the hard-won beauty of becoming. Drawing from a life shaped by hardship, love, loss, and restoration, she writes to tell the truth about what breaks us, what carries us, and what helps us begin again. Her work speaks to women finding their voice, honoring their story, and choosing hope for what comes next.

Morgan Boyd

You're only twelve now—small, your strength nowhere to be found.
The problems you've been through, the situations you've felt that have grown profound.
The four walls that make you feel entrapped, something that you couldn't quite adapt to.
I remember the lonesome feeling of dread, the days you wished you were dead; The thoughts that had filled your head.
The dark, lonesome nights, only wanting to reach for that light.
Wanting anyone to be your knight in shining armor, but you were smarter.
You knew a fairytale wasn't real
you just wanted—you just needed to heal.
Cold, sharp, metal needles breaking your skin
a slight painful reminder that you thought you couldn't win.
Endless tests, each with its own different weight to bear
Wires wrapped—your head, chest, everywhere.
Seizure after seizure,
which left you enduring the endless procedures.
Sitting there staring at the walls in the hospital,
never had you felt so little.
In the enclosed room, with each breath
it almost felt like a dance with death.
Thirteen, fourteen, fifteen, then soon you will see,
at eighteen, you'll find the problem was not as big as you thought it to be.
You don't understand the situation now, but as you grow older, the burden will be smaller,
and you'll begin to grow taller.
You'll grow so tall that you'll outstretch the walls
so tall, you can stand over the waterfalls.
As long as you keep your might,
you'll win the fight.

So trust me when I say: Open your chest, let the dark thoughts
seep out,
you'll be stronger, and once more, your sunlight will finally
break out

Morgan Boyd is an undergraduate student at the University of South Carolina Sumter. She has always found a passion for poetry, but never started writing it until her first semester in college. Her first poem was about writing to her younger self, whom was very depressed and dealing with epilepsy constantly, which is what her poem is about—her battle with her disease. Originally, she was very hesitant to even consider writing a poem for this book, constantly doubting that it would even get recognized. But after the acceptance and from the support from others, she continues to write poetry and has currently won first place in a poetry contest that was held by the Wanda-Hendricks-Bellamy Student Leadership Conference. Considering this book and the contest as two wins, Morgan will remain to write poetry as she goes through life.

Candice Daquin

A better version of tomorrow

I remember you.

15 years old. Angry behind the smile.

I remember you.

Didn't think you could break your heart at 15. Learned you could.

That 15-year-old version of yourself? She didn't think for a moment she'd turn into me. How can I be so sure? What if I'm just remembering it wrong. Except I'm not. I'm remembering it the way you did. 15 isn't so long ago. I was there just yesterday.

Dear 15, you didn't see it because how could you? A feminist sure, but did you know you'd be attacked and left for dead in an alley? Did you imagine how you'd have an abortion, rather than the soft-concept of being 'for' the rights of women? I'm proud of you when I think of your fierceness. The anger you felt at the Guns & Roses poster depicting a woman who looked like she'd been raped. You didn't think one day it would be you, but you imagined it enough to feel outrage. Good on you.

15, you hadn't had the shit kicked out of you yet, but I remember the days you didn't stop crying, the loneliness you felt, the isolation. I wish I could have been a big sister to you. I wish I could have affected your trajectory so you didn't make the same choices I made. I love you in that way I imagine a sibling loves. Neither of us would know what that really felt like. We're both only-children.

When I imagine you now, it's not so hard; you're the indistinct movement from the corner of my eye. The one who was free of today's worries, but you had your own. I loved how bullet-proof youth made you. Bold and sexually free, you were alive in ways I am not. I've grown and I'm proud of that, but I love you for your incompleteness. Whoever said being whole was everything, didn't know.

You cried more than I cry. I am quieter than you. You were a chatter-box, an extrovert, but you masked a lot of the time, something I didn't understand then. It wasn't easy for you, and I hate that, but you didn't let anything stop you. Maybe that's what we share. I don't give up either. We're both Thursday's Child, far to go. I'm just more tired and jaded about it.

If we were best-friends, which I think we would be, or is that the ultimate form of narcissism? I'd protect you. I'd tell you to dump every single person you dated at 15, 16, 17 and beyond. I'd remind you to keep swimming 3 times a week. I'd convince you not to take up smoking. You come from a family of women who smoked, half of whom died of it. Your nihilism became my fear, it's not worth it, you're not cool, you're a fool about that. I'd tell you not to drink until you passed out, even if it did take the pain away. Abuse doesn't leave us, I still have it, but it's easier now to bear, and I don't have to drink to shut it out. You didn't either, you did it because deep-down you were shy, and that's where I can help you. Want to know the secret? None of us survive this thing called life, we all die! So don't feel inferior, none of us will be here in 100 years. Not a single living soul under the age of ten at least.

If you heard me say that; you'd make some wise-crack about robotics or human-hybrids. We were both such Sci-Fi fans. We like the same books still, the same music, but I wouldn't dress like you anymore. It's not the 90's and anyway that was a bad time in fashion. At least it was an era, you'd retort. Not like the 2000's—what's their era? You have a point of course. You were always a fast-thinker.

15, I'd tell you not to sweat the little stuff. Study more. Have faith. All those teachers who told you that you wouldn't make it were wrong. They didn't understand you had a learning disability in math, there was no name for it back then, there is now. Don't let them tear you down, they were wrong. You did great. Because you never gave up. Now you're me and you still don't give up. It's something to be proud of, both of us.

Don't go to America though. I know it'll be hard to say no. It will break hearts. But don't do it. You'd spend years out of status because it was before marriage-equality. Yeah, eventually it does happen, but too late for you. You'll spend years not being able to drive or further your career because you had to be a secret. It was worth it for you and your wife, but it cost too much. Don't break your heart for years on end. Be strong and say no to being a secret. Find another path. The universe is full of them and some hurt less.

I know this will change your trajectory and you won't end up as me, but that's not a bad thing. I'm all right but you could do more. When I say more, I don't mean career, you can't live for that, don't make that mistake either. I mean be more in terms of people. You can have a tribe. You can be part of something. Instead of being the fringe-gay who can't meet her wife's parents, who has to spend Xmas alone, who watches her parent age and forget her because she's 3000 miles away. These are things we didn't think about at 15, why should we? But they catch up with you.

When you go swimming this Saturday, think of me a little? I'm far down the road and I can see you as if it was yesterday. You worried about stretch-marks but you were beautiful. You had dreams that I no longer have, and I want you to realize them. When you dive in the deep-end and for a moment you feel scared, hold onto that fear and let it propel you into a better future than mine. I'm not ungrateful, but I can see multi-universes for you and I love you, so I want something more for you.

I didn't have children, you're probably not surprised, you didn't want them. What will surprise you is how much I grew to want children, but by then it was too late. Reconsider my choices, to give yourself a chance at something more. I care about you as if you were the child I didn't have. Because you are so young. Standing there by the pool, thinking of a boy who will go on to break your heart. I love you and I want you to stay, shining beneath mid-day sun, your undamaged skin and bright eyes. I won't tell you everything that happens down the road because I'm hoping you'll listen to me and some of the things that happened to me, won't happen to you.

Let me imagine you then; not sexually assaulted, not needing a hysterectomy at 32, not hiding when your partners parents come into town. Not miles from where you came from, a stranger in a strange land. I imagine you loved. Because I know you can be, even as you didn't believe it then. I imagine you standing up for yourself and not letting your mother condemn you every time she called. I imagine you believing in yourself earlier than I did, and making something of that. I imagine you being loved without secrecy. I imagine you having friends who understood you, rather than being 3000 miles away, sitting at tables you weren't invited to.

When your dad gets older and forgetful, I think you will remind him and because you spent so many more years together, he will remember. You will still be resilient, and shining, and I will be so proud of you, just for being who you are. I didn't really know it then, did I? But I love you. I tried to protect you best I could, but this is the greatest gift I can give you Candy. Please take me seriously. Please. I just want you to be saved from some of the pain I have felt, some of the disappointment. You didn't do anything wrong, neither of us did. But sometimes we go down the wrong road and we can't see it until it's too late. It isn't too late. Hear me. I see you now, that favorite orange dress, cycling in the rain, you're wonderful. Let me help you save yourself into a better version of tomorrow. I promise you; you won't regret it.

PS: If I haven't said it enough, whatever you decide… even if you end up exactly like me? I'm still proud of you. Because I know exactly what it took to get here. You've done great.

Candice Daquin (she/her) is Managing Editor with Lit Fox Books (Austin, TX). She is a mixed-race immigrant to America, where she's worked as a trauma therapist and writer/editor. Her debut novel, The Cruelty, based on a legacy of sexual violence, was published in the Fall of 2025 (FlowerSong Press).

Gabriella Sofia Meditz

A Love Letter to a much Younger Gabby:

I'm writing to you from a future you can't imagine yet—though, knowing you, you're imagining aliens or some dramatic plot twist. Sorry to disappoint, but the truth is we just... grew up. I'm twenty-one in my final semester of college. (Wilder than the aliens, honestly). I was thinking a lot about you last weekend. I went to our high school's junior retreat again—this time as an alumna leading a group with a senior student. I was the "adult" in the room, looked up to by the students, and asked for advice. It all still feels surreal. I met a girl named Olivia, who reminds me of you—always trying to hide her feelings, pretending not to be a sensitive soul. Spoiler Alert: We still are sensitive. But now, we let it show.

Let's clear some other things up: all the things that you think make you weird? They become things you grow to love and appreciate.

1. Your curly hair will no longer feel like a full-time burden.

2. Your Puerto Rican and Slovenian roots, heritages that dance to two totally different rhythms, will learn to coexist in your bones like a beautifully mismatched duet. One side teaches you warmth, music, flavor, and laughter so loud it rattles the windows. The other teaches you resilience, quiet strength, and the kind of stubbornness that could out-stare a mountain. You're a remix of the two, and you don't even know how lucky you are to be yet.

3. I'm not going to lie to you about the hard things, because you deserve honesty. Loss will come. It will start with Brooke leaving this world earlier than you want, and it will feel like someone dimmed the lights in your life. For a long time, you'll be angry. Then, your grandmothers will leave too. All of their voices will echo in you for years—soft, steady syllables that you'll replay in the quiet moments. You'll carry their stories the way that people carry heirlooms: not fragile, but sacred.

4. Watching mom battle cancer in high school will change the architecture of your heart. You'll learn what real bravery looks like—not the loud, heroic kind, but the kind that shows up in hospital rooms, in repeated prayers, in mornings when you choose hope even when it feels absolutely ridiculous. You'll realize that love is not just something you feel—it's something you do, over and over, even when your hands are shaking.

And yet, in the middle of all this heaviness, life will hand you moments of absurd humor—because apparently the universe thinks emotional whiplash builds character. You'll cry one moment and laugh so hard it hurts the next, sometimes for no reason other than the fact you exist in a body with the coordination of a newborn giraffe. (Yes, this persists. No, you never really do "grow out of it.")

You'll feel lost for a while. Out of place, without purpose. Volunteering with people with disabilities in Esopus will become perhaps one of the brightest threads in your story. You'll really start to see joy in its purest form. You'll learn that connection is not always about having the right words, but about showing up. About listening. About letting your heart soften in the presence of someone else's truth.

Through it all, you will become someone who feels deeply—sometimes too deeply, if we are being honest—but who never hardens. You'll carry love like your grandmothers did, courage like your mom does, and compassion like the work you give your heart to.

And listen, Gab: you willlll mess up. Big time. Often. You will say the wrong thing, trust the wrong person, wear just downright tragic outfits that will haunt you in future photographs, and think your entire life is over roughly 333 times. But each time, you'll get back up. Maybe not gracefully. Maybe after an emotional snack. But you get up.

What you can't see yet is that your life will not just happen to you—you will shape it. With laughter, with grief, with love. With that stubborn, tender heart that refuses to quit. You are becoming someone who will look back on you not with resentment or embarrassment (okay, maybe a little embarrassment), but with so much pride it feels like sunlight. Someone who honors where they come from and who they love and what they've survived. Someone who understands that, much like a glow stick, sometimes we shine brightest after breaking open.

So, keep going. Keep being strange and curious and loud and quiet and everything in between. Dance between cultures, walk through grief, love boldly, stumble often, and choose joy wherever you can find it.

Your life won't ever be easy, but it will be breathtaking.

With much love and a slightly better fashion sense,

Gabby from the future

Gabriella Sofia Meditz (she/her) is a recent graduate of the University of Scranton, where she earned a degree in English. She is preparing to begin Hunter College's dual certification master's program in Education and Deaf and Hard of Hearing Studies this spring. A lover of poetry, memoirs, and long runs, Meditz turns to writing as a way of paying attention–to language, to silence, and to the many forms communication can take. Her work is rooted in curiosity, care, and the belief that stories have the power to connect, teach, and endure.

Armethia Sims

Dear 24-year-old Armethia,

You go, girl! You have joined the ranks of dreamers like John Lennon and Dr. Martin Luther King. You will have more appreciation of your stances in life when you see that over the next 55 years, how your stance in April 1970 has exemplified the American people's actions that have kept this country free. You believed that you and the young people of this nation could change the world.

Within five decades, you will clearly see reports of peaceful and non-peaceful protests on the streets in this country and other countries that made great changes happen. These events are reminiscent of the 1960s and early 1970s, when there were protests for civil rights, women's rights, and anti-war efforts. Young folks like you were considered idealistic dreamers, and even some called you a militant (wearing your big natural Afro hairstyle), particularly when you got arrested in an anti-war protest at Miami University in Oxford, Ohio, in April of 1970.

There were a few precursors that affected your anti-war thoughts.

As a Black teenager growing up in the small city of Middletown, Ohio, you gained most of your knowledge about worldly affairs from books, magazines, or television. You read Ebony and Jet, magazines which were Black-owned and informative about Black issues, celebrities, and the rest of Black Americans, especially in the fight for equal rights. Television showed you civil rights protesters being watered down with hoses, & beaten to the ground. You always wondered why it had to be this way. You had learned most of our Black history from church and our grandmother, so you were aware of how we got to this point, but why was there still so much hate?

Then came the Vietnam War, in which young Black men were being drafted way out of proportion to the rest of the male population. During this time, you attended part-time a Miami

University extension branch in Middletown and worked various jobs to pay for your education. You were 22 years old before you transferred to the main campus.

By April of 1970, you knew guys who were drafted out of college and sent to Vietnam. The MyLai massacre had occurred. The war became unpopular on campuses across the country. You were always against the war, but after a young family friend named Steve enlisted, you felt more strongly about whether this was a relevant war for this country to send men to die. Steve was the neighborhood newspaper boy. He always delivered our papers to the door, smiling and speaking very mannerly. Everyone knew him and his family. When he had just graduated from high school, Steve was forced to enlist by a local judge. A fatal shooting of a White teenager by a Black teenager had happened during a fight at a local club, and Steve fit the description of the Black teen. He was arrested and arraigned, but there wasn't enough evidence for it to go to trial. Steve's family was too poor to get a lawyer, so all he could have was a public defender, who did nothing for him. The judge offered Steve the deal of the judge dropping all the charges if Steve enlisted in the army. This was not uncommon at that time for this to happen to Black males. Steve enlisted and was soon killed in Vietnam.

His father reported to our family that Steve's back was blown off. Later, the boy who really did the shooting was found. You turned totally against war. Four of our brothers had been serving in World War II when you were born, but you still became very anti-war. You thought there must be a way to solve the issues of the world without killing one another.

On April 15, 1970, you were walking across Miami University's campus and noticed a large crowd of hundreds of students inside and around the Air Force ROTC building. There was loud music coming from the inside. When you walked over to the building, you realized the students had taken over the building. One of the football players you knew was playing his conga drum & other students had musical instruments playing inside the building. There was a speaker with a megaphone speaking anti-war rhetoric. When you went inside, several students that you knew well were participating, and one was your roommate from Middletown. You all were partying in the building until the Dean of Students showed up with campus security, ordering everyone out. They had called the county sheriff and state police. Everyone immediately locked arms and sat on the floor.

As the Dean threatened to arrest and take students' financial aid, academic and athletic scholarships, many started getting up and leaving the building. You stayed with about 200 students and got arrested. As the Black students witnessed how law officers grabbed the White students by their long hair and dragged them across the floor, even hitting some of them, you all said to each other, "If they'll do that to Whites, what will they do to us?"

Some fear did creep in, but you were determined to stay steadfast. The black students locked arms and decided that if you all were going down, then you would go down together. The Dean tried to convince the Black students that this was not their fight and brought in other Black staff to talk you all out of the protest, but the Black staff backed the students when they saw the strong determination and gave the students an upward fist salute.

At that point, the Dean motioned for the police to continue arresting everyone. The police didn't beat the black students, but you were among seven Black students arrested and jailed. All seven of you were bailed out the next morning by a couple of Black graduate students, who had gone to the university staff soliciting bail money. You were with about 40 of the women who were jailed in cells located in the male part of the county jail because they didn't have enough room in the women's section. It had become night when they packed all the women in the jail cells like sardines in a can. Everyone had to find spaces on the floor to sit. As the night progressed, some of the women talked and shared feelings, while others slept in awkward positions.

You remember one girl spoke of discrimination by a professor because she was a female who wanted to go to medical school, and he told her she would take up space that would be better for a male. Others spoke about the senseless war. You expressed hope that with so many protests around the country, maybe

the president would end the war and bring the guys home, but another girl, who was very despondent, said, "You are dreaming." She didn't even want to bring kids into this world because of the direction it was going.

Many shared their feelings about the treatment of non-White, poor people and women in this country. You said as long as there is life, there is hope. The women expressed their feelings until they fell asleep. All of the protesters were kicked out of Miami University until disciplinary hearings were held.

Even though some people thought the country was going to hell, you were a follower of Dr. Martin Luther King's dream, and you imagined a world where all could live together in equality and peace. That coming year, John Lennon came out with the song

Imagine. "Imagine all the people living life in peace." You loved the lyrics.

After your hearings, most of you were let back in school, except the guys who broke the lock on the ROTC building. The Seniors who were in the school of education, of which you were one, were told by the disciplinary committee that they would let you all graduate, but you would not be allowed to get a teaching license in the state of Ohio. That really threw you for a loop. You were already scheduled to student teach in Cleveland's inner city that coming Fall, so you didn't know the point of doing that if you could not become a teacher.

A friend who lived in upstate New York called you and told you about a Summer job working with the children of migrant workers in upstate New York. Children under 14 could not be pickers in the field, so a day program was created with activities for the kids, while their parents picked apples and cherries in the fields. You worked that Summer job, and before the Summer was over, the American Civil Liberties Union sent you a letter letting you know you could student-teach in the Fall and receive your teaching licensure because they had sued the university, and the university backed off.

You did get to become a teacher. You married and went to graduate school in counseling, and eventually became a mental health therapist. In 2022, a Miami University professor in the Communications department produced a documentary of the 1970 protest and commemorated all of you. The documentary is on the Miami University website, with you and other former Miami anti-war protesters being interviewed.

At 80 years old, I now look back and recognize that you did and continue to stand up for your values and beliefs. You helped to make me the woman that I am. John Lennon said, "You can say I'm a dreamer, but I'm not the only one". Be glad to join the ranks of dreamers like Lennon and Dr. King, and all dreamers who are not as notable as these two men. Be grateful for desiring the world to be as ONE!. Be grateful for all the young protesting students of those times, (especially the females), because for the next

55 years to come, other than voting, or boycotting, non-violent protests will remain one of the major means used to keep our democracy. Keep on keeping on.

Love forever,

Armethia

Armethia Sims is a retired mental Health therapist, who has also worked as a high school teacher & counselor. Previously a resident of Michigan, she has also been a member of the Ann Arbor, Michigan Women Artists Association. Armethia moved from Michigan to Leesburg, VA, five years ago to be near her daughter & grandchildren. She has always loved to express her creativity through artwork, and has now become interested in learning to use her writing creativity after taking a class with facilitator Diana Diehl at the Leesburg Senior Center. Having lived for 80 years, Armethia, like most Seniors, has many life experiences to share in written memoir form.

Photo courtesy of author.

Sarah Josephine Pennington

Letter to my twenties--
after Pauletta Hansel

Listen, girl,
your life
is going
to lead
you in
so many
directions.

Some forks you'll choose
careful as a bride selecting
wedding silver,

sometimes the brakes will go out,
sudden—
in the runaway car of your life and
you'll white knuckle your way

fast

into the unknown,
chasing your own tail
into uncharted lands that will become,
eventually,
the places you will call home,

places you will know, not like the back of your hand,
maybe,
but well enough for them to remain frozen
in your dreams, familiar as an old kmart—
gone for years now, but imprinted forever,
familiar as a toothache.

Just like your tongue can find
the sore spot of a cavity

even after it's been carefully filled,
just like you could walk through those
blue light special doors if they appeared again and find
your way to the milk, the cassette tapes, the socks,
you'll learn your way around these new places
until the unknown unknowns of them
become part of you,
until even the dark of them becomes,
through some trick of time and age and too much heart,
a source of nostalgia,
a comfortable revelry
when you're settled in greener lands.

Sarah Josephine Pennington (she/her) is a queer writer and artist from Louisville, KY by way of Appalachia. Her work has appeared or is forthcoming in journals including Still: The Journal, Salvation South, and Pine Mountain Sand and Gravel.

Letters of Witness to the Present

Ambition scares them.
Who knew success could trigger
So much fragile rage?

But from where I'm writing … the next chapter—your next chapter—is the good one.

-Leslie Frisbee

Tracy Shaw

Dearest one,

As I sit in my easy chair, listening to the rain, watching what's left of the daylight slip away by 4:30, I wonder, however did I get here? I think back to a conversation that Tim and I had early on in our relationship. We were sitting on my front porch talking and he asked me, "What are your goals?"

It had always been my goal to be married, settled, and have children by thirty, but instead I was going through a divorce, just me and my Bassett hound. I had to really think about my answer. What do I want? Do I have the same dreams now? I remember answering, "I want to travel." I had never really been outside of the southeast United States, except for a trip to Cancun. After some hesitation, I also said, "I do still want a family. I want children and a husband to share life with."

Those goals, Dear One, don't give up on them! Listen to your heart. Be true to yourself even when times get tough and the timelines you set are not met. Two weeks ago, I was able to see the Eiffel Tower in all its glory. We were coming into dock after an afternoon cruise on the Seine. Just as we were unloading beyond the base of the tower, the clock struck 18.00, and the Eiffel... Well, the Eiffel, she sparkled. She glowed. She lit the night sky. She put on a wonderful show for us and when it was over she stood tall, strong, and glowed from her internal lights.

Remember your own internal lights, Schatz. Learn how to fuel them. Feed them so they become bright and strong. Pay no attention if others don't see the same value you do. Just keep doing what you know to be right. But, Dearest One, don't forget to rest. Be sure to listen to your body and give it what it needs both spiritually and physically. Those lights can't shine if you ignore your body.

The daylight is ending here and soon I too must rest. For in a few days our youngest is joining us here in Delmenhorst. She has plans; a soccer match in Leipzig, a visit to Gröningen, Thanksgiving with family friends in Oerlinghausen, Munich with a trip to Salzburg thrown in, and I want to be available for it all! So, see, hang on to those dreams, and let go of timelines because what matters most is not when, or if, you accomplish your goals, but the love and effort you put in on the journey.

Much love to you,
Tracy

Tracy Shaw (she/her) is a retired educator, living in Columbia, SC, who fulfills her joy by continuing to work with children, volunteering as a tutor at Rosewood Elementary School. She has a passion for travel and has lived for extended periods in Germany. Tracy currently finds joy in dirt therapy in her garden, sewing, knitting, exercise classes at the Lourie center, and attending Good Shepherd Episcopal Church. Writing is actually not one of her passions!

Patricia Hatch

Dear Patricia,

Please become the uncontainable, gray-haired woman in our dreams. Whatever you do, hold tight to her. I beg of you. She's fabulously regal, if still a figment of our imagination. I know you know her, because she stares fiercely back at us when we close our eyes, a mirror of ourselves in years to come.

She's the woman held in high esteem, but who hugs generously. Who speaks with a gravity capable of hushing a full room. Her mother's intelligent, quiet image, her father's overflowing spirit. Who loves wildly and unrestrained, enfolding people into the layers of her tapestry. She keeps plants in windows and drinks tea. Takes vitamins and stretches daily. Curses, but sparingly. Welcomes friends who walk through doors without knocking. Our white-haired self wears flowy linen, really pajamas masquerading as refinement. All dressed up with jewelry, she smells faintly of incense.

But mainly, please become her, because it means we escaped this box we keep building without intention. There are days when we get lost in our thoughts, those dangerous moments when we allow ourselves space to dream. When hope seems a tad desperate, and we can't quite silence the vague yearning. Right now, I can't let her out or give her space to stretch, because.

What if she gets extinguished before she even turns her face to the sun?

It's as if the universe calls to her from a distance, an echo indiscernible still, and so. Someday, when our silver-haired self gazes back—bright eyes piercing a lifetime of journeys—inviting us in, please say yes. Good God, she loves to play the hymns, and she's taught them all to you, so sit down. Just make sure that this time—

You Stay.

Peace and love,
Patricia

Patricia Hatch (she/her) is an educator, musician, and writer. For decades, she has kindled her passion for the humanities and arts through teaching, learning alongside her students. Patricia finds inspiration in all walks of nature, often visiting local greenways or escaping to the woods for a sense of clarity; she currently resides in North Carolina.

Nathalie Kaupp

Dear my 20 something year old self,

Confidence, self worth, independence in mind and body, love for God, for your husband, and for yourself is what you will grow up to have.

You will not attain this until your late 30's and early 40's. The career you wanted will not be the job you have, but you will be happy and content. The family you thought loved you will be the mirror image of the reality they represented. You will fight for your freedom, and with God by your side, you will win.

Yes, I said God. For though your faith has slipped, you will find it again in your darkest moments. He leads you to your destiny and to the future you make with him. You think the future is set. That no matter what you try at you will fail, so why bother?

It is not. Life is like the leaves on a tree–always changing. You have to be like the wind blowing through the leaves, ebbing and flowing. No matter the obstacle, finding your way around and through. Your future becomes what you make of it with God's guidance in everything you do.

Love,

Your 43 year old self

Nathalie Ashley Kaupp (she/her) was born in California and raised in Charleston, South Carolina. She has a Film Production Certificate and a BA in Film Studies. Nathalie has volunteered with ETV, written film articles for a news blog, and been a shelver for two libraries. She currently serves as a substitute teacher and after-care co-manager for a Catholic high school during the week and an Episcopal parish on Sundays. She lives in Columbia, SC, with her husband and pets.

Leslie Frisbee

Dear You,

You're still small enough to hang from the uneven bars without your hands sweating, so let me start there: you don't know it yet, but you're already training for the real act—the one where you spend a lifetime trying to be "your best," chasing some invisible judge whose scorecard you will never actually see.

You'll get A's, medals, ribbons. You'll be a gymnast, a runner, a cheerleader who can smile through a pulled muscle and a dance rehearsal gone sideways. The grown-ups will clap and say things like *You work so hard* and *You're such a perfectionist*, and it will sound like praise because everyone around you treats it like praise. No one will tell you that perfection is a bottomless pit with excellent lighting.

You'll hold yourself to standards that impressed even the adults who set them, but still, you will look in the mirror and not quite believe any of it. You'll feel too big, too small, too something, and because you're good at following instructions, you'll try to shrink the parts you think take up too much room. That will become its own quiet war—one you'll fight while smiling for the camera, while editing stories late at night, while pretending you're fine because people like girls who are fine.

Meanwhile, you will rise. You'll rise in an industry that still struggles to recognize women as fully human, never mind ambitious. You'll write your way into rooms where you once imagined only men could sit. You'll cover legends. You'll build magazines. You'll shape cultural conversations before you realize that's what you're doing. And you'll spend an embarrassing amount of time wondering if someone made a clerical error when they let you through the door.

People will love your ambition when it benefits them. They will resent it when it doesn't. The men who seem supportive will occasionally turn out to be the ones who test your boundaries the hardest. The women who smile at you in meetings will not always be the ones cheering for you when the lights go down. And you—God love you—will keep trying to be the "good" one, the hardworking one, the one who earns every inch of space she takes up. You will think if you just do your job well enough, you'll be safe. This turns out to be adorable.

You will be one of the early voices in what will later be called #MeToo. You won't think of yourself that way at the time—you'll just think you're telling the truth. You will not be prepared for how many people prefer the lie. Some will twist the story. Some will vanish. Some will do what cowards always do: blame the messenger. You'll get knocked down in ways that are unfair, and devastating, and unforgettable. And yes—women will be among the loudest. That betrayal will cut differently. You'll learn from it, but you won't grow bitter. (This will annoy people, too.)

Here's what matters: you will survive every single blow. Better than that—you'll rebuild. You won't do it all at once. Reinvention arrives the way spring does in the Midwest: in tiny, stubborn hints. You'll return to school. You'll rediscover your voice by using it on your own terms. You'll start to examine your life with more generosity than judgment. You'll write a book about this season—how we're taught to chase our achievements like survival rations, only to discover that reinvention isn't about triumph at all. It's about clarity. It's about finally knowing what belongs to you and what never did.

You will learn that "enough" is not a consolation prize. It is the whole point.

And then—and I cannot stress this enough—just when you think the universe is done handing out plot twists, you'll get one so tailored, so absurdly specific to your talents and your history, that you will laugh. A dream job. A job you might have sketched in a notebook if you ever believed you were allowed to want something that big. A job that feels like God leaned over the drafting table and said, "This one. For her. She's ready now."

You will be. But only because of everything that came before: the medals you earned, the ones you starved for, the newsroom battles you won, the ones you lost, the women who underestimated you, the men who tried to derail you, the seasons where you felt used up, the mornings you still got up anyway. You'll carry all of that into this new chapter—not as weights, but as tools. As proof that reinvention isn't a makeover; it's a decision.

The truth is, younger you wouldn't have believed any of this. You were too busy trying to fit into a world that never quite knew what to do with women like you. Let me save you some time: your voice will be your superpower. Your intuition will be your shield. Your resilience will be the part people don't see until they push too hard and it pushes back.

And grace—real grace—is what you will learn after you lose the things you were sure defined you.

Here's the secret no one told you: nothing you do will ever make you "enough" if you don't decide that you already are. You will spend years learning this. You will spend the rest of your life practicing it.

But from where I'm writing, I can tell you this with absolute certainty:

You make it. You more than make it.

And the next chapter—your next chapter—is the good one.

Love,

Your Future Self

Leslie Frisbee (she/her) is a journalist, editor, and writer who has spent more than 20 years in the luxury lifestyle space, covering culture, travel, and the people behind it. Her work has been recognized by the Nevada Press Association and Writer's Digest. She is currently completing The Other Side of June, a literary collection focused on reinvention and the complicated work of becoming yourself.

Jo Angela Edwins

Notes to My Younger Self

That boy you had a crush on in high school
will never date you, but he'll grow up
to be a good, kind man.

That man your sister secretly married
because the white south still could not stand
her love for a black man will nonetheless leave her
for another woman before you finish high school.
You will wonder if it's because of the secret.
Your sister will chase him. You will worry your parents
will find out the truth and disown her.
You will worry in your self-absorbed confusion
that you will never see her again.
Your parents, it seems, never find out.
Your sister never gets a divorce, even after
the last time she sees him, a day you'll never know
the date of. Years later, you will believe
your parents knew all along but chose silence
over bravery, or pain. Just like you.

That man you'll love madly for a decade
will never be able to love you back the way
anyone deserves. One night, years later, when you live
two states away, he will call you and mumble
through a bourbon haze, "I wish I could have fallen
completely in love with you." You will say,
"Well, you didn't." Years later, when he dies,
you'll grieve hard the good things about him.
You'll fight hard against valorizing the dead
and constantly remind yourself of the bad.
Nevertheless, you will never understand
a world in which he doesn't speak or breathe.

That woman who gave birth to you, who will love
you more fiercely than anyone else in your life,

will die too young, when you are far away.
She will appear in your dreams smart and eager
to drive off into the graying distance.
Nothing you say will keep her at home. You will
awaken thinking she's somewhere in the room.

That man who angered you as a child
because a father shouldn't ruin holidays
drunkenly screaming will eventually quit drinking,
will survive heart attacks and embolism,
will grow old by growing kinder in his words
even as his memory clouds. He will die
alone in a hospice room one night in the dead
of winter. You will be the last child
he sees before he dies, and still you'll wish
for the rest of your life you'd been in his room that night.

This or that friend will share deep confidences,
choking laughs, bottles of liquor, desserts,
and then will whisper behind your back, or leave you
stranded on the highway, or call you bitch,
or do nothing of the sort but still will move
hundreds of miles away and gradually
won't answer a text or return the favor
of a holiday card, and soon enough
you'll think of them less and less, and it will be
OK, until one day it isn't, and you'll cry.

That person you are now—young, strong, quick-minded—
will become what now you think of as stooped and old,
but she won't think that way. She'll want to stir
heat into every sauce, she'll want to wear
those shoes you never dared to when you could,
she'll want to flaunt and flirt and shout at stars,
and she'll know the world will laugh, but she will do
what she wants to, what she can. She will wish
you'd had the guts, young goddess, to do the same.
And most of all, she'll want to shout, you will be fine,
you will be fine, you will be fine, dear girl, yes, fine.

Don't quiver in corners, because this much you'll learn:
you will be fine, fine, fine, yes, woman, just fine.

Jo Angela Edwins (she/her) has published poems in over 100 journals and anthologies, including Pirene's Fountain, New South, Whale Road Review, and The Hollins Critic. She is the author of the collection A Dangerous Heaven (2023) and the chapbooks Bitten (2025) and Play (2016). She serves as the poet laureate of the Pee Dee region of South Carolina and is the coordinator of Creative Writing at Francis Marion University.

Letters of Reclamation

You can wear the short shorts if you want to.

-Dory Maguire

I remember who I am. Worthy. Radiant. Resilient. Irreplaceable.

I no longer shrink to fit into spaces I have outgrown. All parts of me are welcome here.

-MaryAddison Yates

Dory Maguire

Anti-silhouette Recognition Wardrobe

You can wear the cute shorts
if you want to.
Don't worry about the
lustful male gaze or what
the judgmental female says.
You can wear a tight shirt
that shows your curves;
you don't have to shroud
yourself in a billowing monstrosity
of convex silhouette distortion.
This bulk that you carry is your armor.
I declare the war over;
I declare the world safe,
because we all wish it so.

Dory Maguire (she/her) is the author of five self-published collections of poetry, each illustrated with her original photography. Dory's poems have received multiple honorable mentions in the National Federation of State Poetry Societies' annual contests and appear in several anthologies. A committed advocate for poets, Dory hosted her local poetry workshop on her patio during the pandemic when library meetings were suspended, and she remains an active presence in the poetry community, supporting small groups and gatherings both in-person and via Zoom. She lives on a horse farm in Pennsylvania, where she spends her free time sprouting trees, tending forests, and drawing inspiration from the land she stewards.

Delia Corrigan

Delia,

Okay. Dear Delia. Okay, okay. Kind Delia. "What did you say your name is? Celia? Oh, you said Delia. That's such a pretty name." It was my dad's mother's name. Hushed stories about Grandmother Delia the grown-ups wouldn't explain. Those seeds silently maturing in dark, nourishing DNA. Her whispered struggles mine—what is *karma*, anyway? I'll look it up. I love words.

It is Sunday morning, and I'm propped up by three pillows and no intention of formal, shared worship. I stare and stare out of my favorite beach window. I've grown up with this palmetto palm, now so large I can reach out and touch its many textures. This morning, this is my worship. A memory beckons like the soft blue of sky peeking between fans of green fronds and old brown growth that needs to be cleared out.

You're at your desk with attached chair, too big for your knobby-kneed frame. You've picked from the seating chart a space near the long window, cranked open from the bottom. It's "Maymester" in Mrs. Whitehouse's classroom, seventh grade, the first year you were allowed to choose an elective. Three weeks of Latin, Greek mythology and English vocabulary, a twisting funnel of delight. It's after lunch, other students half-dazed, half-dozed, Stefanie doodling on her book's cover, clicking her fat pen of many colors —I'm just trying to stay awake, she tells me. So many bees working patches of clovers outside that there's actually a droning—a sound I remember but haven't heard for many years.

The word *abnegate*. I recently heard that word and I'm back in Vocabulary and Language class. Can my seventh grade self explain to my 60-year-old self why that word fascinated you so, a trance in which I still walk? The melodic sound? The mystery of gods and goddesses testing fate and each other, often with disastrous losses and abnegations? Or maybe simply the word's clear breakdown of meaningful parts, its numerous synonyms with which to construct all manner of sentences. Or was it a liminal, otherworld knowing of what Delia would one day abnegate, and what she wouldn't refuse that she should have?

Well, dear Delia, things, genes, continue to play out and choices continue to be made. Let's sit here together, exposed, staying in our window-light, seeking truth.

Love,

Delia

You use the word *abnegate*
in your poem and take me back
abnegate abnegare abnegation
logos upon logos roll from palate
to tongue, a show of caverned strength

How I chased the language, matched
synonyms, lined antonyms, circled
prefixes with green pen-*ab ab ab*
knifed slashes between syllables, labeled.
Verb. Transitive. Latin origin.   Absorbed in the world of words —
Why did my classmates not relish the mystery?

Seventh-grade self, are you disappointed?
Do your wondering eyes discern what's hidden
from others, what I have *abnegated*—certain parts
of our very soul? Or is this lung-weight
mere common desire for eternal innocence?

Dimensions   dissolve   I'm the third   wheel
at a two person   see saw.   I'm twirling
in new   Patton Sunday shoes.   I'm lying on my paisley
comforter thinking vicious thoughts
about nearly everything, everyone
not yet having a word for   *despair*
already a companion at thirteen.
Reversion. NOUN, the act of going back to a person
or place. Homecoming

Frizzy freckled seventh grade me, may I have this dance?
Shall we?

Delia Corrigan (she/her) has written for The State newspaper; Reach Out, Columbia! Magazine; Lake Murray Magazine; and Columbia Metropolitan Magazine. She is the author of two children's books, The Bad Haircut Day, and Go Team! Mascots of the SEC. Her poetry has been published in Utmost Christian Writers; Alive Now!, Beginnings magazine, Winning Writers, The Comet, Fall Lines, Jasper, The South Carolina Poetry Society newsletter, Hilton Head Poetry Trail, Local Life, Kakalak, and Congaree Anthology. She lives in Columbia, SC.

MaryAddison Yates

Hey Little MA!

I'm writing to let you know we finally found the missing key. Our Key, the one that unlocks our ability to create, shift, change and visit any reality we choose. I can't believe we didn't even know we had misplaced it, and within our very own heart! This is epic and it changes everything. All these years, searching, seeking, desperately trying to answer the riddle of, "What must I do to be worthy of love?" Despite our uncertainty, we ultimately chose to trust our intuition.

You know our earliest memory of Little MA hiding under the three-legged table in the living room, the one that's been haunting us our whole lives? Where you were anticipating the moment when mom, dad or brother would ask "Where's MaryAddison? We can't start the movie without her." Well, my love, this is for you. For all we endured. For all we survived. For all we are still becoming.

Little MA always had the best hiding spots. She'd squeeze into the bathroom cabinets, climb underneath the laundry piles, and quite often, hide in plain sight. She was so good at hiding that sometimes she forgot she hadn't even told anyone to come look for her. She was so creative and lived in so many different realms. Somehow, she accidentally got stuck in an imaginary reality where she believed she had become invisible. Crouched under the three-legged table, she waited—hoping someone would notice she was missing, hoping someone would come.

On the original timeline, she had been trapped in that world for almost 40 years when, during a therapy session, I went back to rescue Little MA from underneath the table. To my surprise, I saw her standing beside the table. She was waiting patiently, ready to be seen, waiting for me to see and receive. She took my hands, looked up at me and beamed. For the first time, I saw our light and it almost took my breath away. My heart filled with warmth and a tingling sensation radiated down my arms, like fireflies being released from in a mason jar. Our love and light flowed all the way down to the tips of my toes, and we were one, able to fully flourish and grow.

It was the most magical moment of my life, but then Big MA got sucked in and was trapped in the realm of Little MA's painful reality. While she had been reunited and reintegrated with Little MA, she didn't know that she needed to lock that world down with The Key. Stuck in the in-between, frantically looking everywhere outside herself to escape, she was opening portals to realities in several different areas of her life. Everything was open halfway; she was disoriented and weary because she had not yet remembered that she held The Key to escape.

Big MA was trapped in the in-between for more than four years until one day during a meditative journey she entered the portal in which it was left. She entered through door number 7 and found herself in a beautiful forest. Shortly after she started walking, she came to a clearing with a lamp post that reminded her of the land of Narnia. It was eerily quiet, like all the animals were holding their breath anticipating the evil Snow Queen. She proceeded with caution and soon came to a small structure made of stone. She walked around the outside and wasn't sure whether it was abandoned but decided to go inside anyway. At first it was dark and then she saw a family of spotted leopards gathered around a fireplace in the den. They seemed warm and loving towards each other. The childhood memory of Little MA in the den, hiding under the table started to surface. As it did, she noticed one of the cubs started to wander off when mama leopard lovingly brought her back to the rest of the family. She got the sense that this cub wandered off alone out of curiosity and a desire to explore vs. Little MA's experience of isolation.

Suddenly, everything went white. She felt a sense of danger like there was about to be an invasion or an attack. A few feet ahead, an object on a single pedestal started to appear. It was gold and round, almost like the combination of a compass and a Rubik's Cube. It was intriguing and it instinctually felt important, so she picked it up. The moment she did, it felt at home, her whole body exhaled with relief. All of the sudden, she was startled by the vision of multiple logging trucks speeding down a highway headed directly towards the forest. Just before impact, her reality abruptly switched again. She was trapped inside a computer screen with thousands of algorithms running vertically with no end in sight. As she held the object in her hand and observed the changing realms, she sensed it had the ability to shift realities across multiple timelines and dimensions. She intuitively understood it was extremely important that this object did not fall into the wrong hands. There were too many different combinations, possible outcomes and unknowns to leave up to chance.

Door number 7 started to come into Big MA's vision, and she knew this journey was coming to an end. She was torn whether to leave the shape shifting object but sensed it needed her protection. Right before she was about to exit, she took it and hid it in the first place she thought of—her heart. Not for possession, as an act of reclamation. Not for manipulation, but for manifestation. Our truth restored—together, we create the reality of our choosing. She closed the door, sealed it with an "X" and proclaimed, "It is done," and slowly returned to our current time and reality.

The Key has been returned to our heart—never to be forgotten or misplaced again. I remember who I am. Worthy. Radiant. Resilient. Irreplaceable.

I no longer shrink to fit into spaces I have outgrown. All parts of me are welcome here. I am the creator of my reality. I return, I rise, I reign.

And so, it is.

To and from The Key within my heart,
MaryAddison

MaryAddison Yates(she/her) is a writer, speaker, and empowerment coach whose work explores healing, self-worth, and the reclamation of inner truth. Having navigated addiction, identity shifts, and profound personal transformation, she communicated with honesty, tenderness, and clarity. Her work invites people to reconnect with parts of themselves long left unseen and to remember their inherent worth. She lives in South Carolina, where she is raising twins and continuing her own journey of growth and becoming.
More info at https://bio.site/MaryAddison

Patricia Hatch

Dear DLRS,

Yesterday, your big brother called me our nickname, completely cracking himself up. Even now, he refers to you as Dirty Little Rotten Stinker. What a badge of honor our oldest brother has bestowed upon us!

We are bold. Sensitive. Quick. Constantly working with dirty hands, stringy hair, scabbed over knees. A reader. Books often get us in trouble. I know you recently hid under our blanket late at night with a flashlight to read Nancy Drew, only to overhear our parents do the deed. You couldn't look at them the next day!

Occasionally sneaky. Only-child-kind of selfish. (Sharing can prove challenging sometimes. Especially cookies and pencils.) Mom's mini me. Dad's partner in crime. Your sister's shadow. Your youngest brother's sidekick. Your much older siblings' rag doll for sport. Spoiled in the right ways, including junk food just because. Passionate. Daydreamer. Mrs. Dent wrote on your permanent record that you stare out the window and you're bossy, by the way. You love her, but she has your number.

Tree climber. That willow tree could be counted in your list of best friends, the way you stand high up in her strong branches, declaring rule over the backyard. There won't be many trees like her in your future, but hopefully, one day we'll discover her reincarnated soul. Trailblazer. Hiking complainer. Crawdad catcher. Best friend to the Imaginary Jason.

Later, freshman year of college, they will name it ADHD. It's the first test you actually ace since you've arrived. The university adds college success seminars in the attic of the library to your schedule. A label helps you finally understand why you see the world so differently from others and honestly, once you harness it, ADHD becomes your superpower. You even learn how to speed read!

Frankly, hasn't it been exhilarating living outside the boxes so far?

Self Love,

DLRS, Adulting

Patricia Hatch (she/her) is an educator, musician, and writer. For decades, she has kindled her passion for the humanities and arts through teaching, learning alongside her students. Patricia finds inspiration in all walks of nature, often visiting local greenways or escaping to the woods for a sense of clarity; she currently resides in North Carolina.

Liona Burnham

In the Days After an Ultrasound Without a Heartbeat

Dear L,

The last baby, the phantom one
that causes you so much pain
at parks and schools,
she isn't gone,
just waiting.

One summer when the world
goes inside and shuts the doors
she will be born.

You will nurse her
in the living room
and the maple leaves that year
will make a red-yellow-orange roof
as you look through windows.
The house will be quiet
after the hammering is done for the day.
Her sisters will hold her
and gaze into her tiny face.

This wonder will never fully melt.
Even when she is five,
you will look at her
eating toast with jam next to you
and feel sunlight
stream through your body.

Let that quiet grief
that the world says
is for mere flesh, not human,
open you to all that is coming.
Let that grief
that the world says

you shouldn't speak
become a story
because our stories
birth us.

One day you will tell
this story in the dance studio
while the baby dances.
Your friend will cry
and so will you
and it will be good.
You will both say,
it was so long ago.

Liona T. Burnham (she/her) is a poet and professor. She has poems published or forthcoming in The Comstock Review, Allium, Rock Paper Poem, Crab Orchard Review, Sky Island Journal, and more. She teaches at a community college. She lives with her husband, three daughters, two cats, and one hamster in the Pacific Northwest.

Dahlia Fisher

I remember you, girl. A nervous small pudge of a thing, wearing clothes that itched and scratched and made you want to scream. There was nothing to you yet. And yet you cried out at night as if you were being tormented by some kind of deep pain. Your heart sped around the racetrack drumming hard to make the wheels turn fast: be-dum-de-dum, be-dum-de-dum, be-dum-de-dum. What were you trying to outrun? And so young?

I remember how you lay still in your antique bed, tucked under your fluffy feather comforter like a life-size plastic doll. Arms rigid by your side, eyelids flapping open and shut, watching the shadows on your ceiling turn into psychedelic monsters on your walls, and when you called for your mother and father, they came running to your room, and told you that you were fine. So, you learned that this was what it meant to be fine.

This is what I want you to know. You'll grow bigger, and somewhat wiser, and the things that happen to you will look like different things, but they are in fact the same things happening over and over again. You'll see what I mean.

You'll meet the same man dressed in different sheep's clothing. You will trust him, but not yourself. Like a dart board, you will have to be ready at any time to play. But, I remember you. Soft and doughy. You were not made to be hardened or prepared for someone to hit you in the bullseye. Do not be fine. Show all your ugly parts. Be vulgar and naked. Rip off your clothes. Show yourself to yourself. The rolls, the folds, the fat. Be round and real. And scream, scream, scream.

When you meet the givers, hold them close. They will calm you. They will soothe you. Your heart will sound like an ocean drift when they are with you, wu-wah, wu-wah, wu-wah. Clear the radio static in your head, like a prescription. People can be good like antibiotics or bad like heroin. When you're able to think clearly, you can envision beautiful possibilities. You have a gift, girl, you are a gift, girl. But all that noise in your head will make you feel hazy, crazy, lazy, and you'll say you're fine, but don't be fine. Break through it. Scream through it, until the fog clears. Until the shadows disappear. You will be wild before you are free.

You'll spend time in therapy. You'll want to know where this pain comes from and you'll take a shovel to your insides and try dig it out of you like a parasite cut off from its host. But you'll never find the source. Stop looking. Stop searching. There are no answers here. The pain is deep within you, from a time before you were born. It came with you to this earth. Recycled. But it does not belong to you. You want to bury it, but it will try and bury you.

This is what I want you to know. One day you will lay in your bed, staring at the ceiling and instead of monsters you will see me. Out of the shadows, you will be face to face with yourself. Tired of fighting, you'll wonder if you are ready to die. Girl, no, you are not going to die. Your heart is beating, sturdy and steady. Bum-bum, bum-bum, bum-bum.

Through it all, we survive.

Dahlia Fisher (she/her) is a Pushcart Prize-nominated author, produced playwright, and writing instructor based in Cleveland, OH. Her recent accolades include winning the 2023 Etruscan Press Prize and being shortlisted for the 2024 Black Spring Prize. Dahlia's short fiction and creative non-fiction explore the nuances of voice and identity, appearing in publications such as Gordon Square Review, HerStry, and The Land.

Dahlia holds an MFA in Creative Writing, an MA in Communications, and a BA in Theater. Beyond the page, she applies her narrative expertise as Chief Strategist at Hello MOD and fosters literary dialogue as the co-founder of Rebel Readers Cleveland, a cross-cultural community book club.

Letters of Release

Your hair texture isn't frizzy, it's just curly and burnt from that 1970s Sears hairdryer Dad won't throw away.

-Sarah Josephine Pennington

You are not a HUMAN mechanic; you cannot fix people.

-Alicia Harris

Life is like the leaves on a tree—always changing.

-Nathalie Kaupp

You will be fine.

-Jo Angela Edwins

Your definition of success will change.

-D. Nichole Davis

You will be fine.

-Mare Schumacher

Catherine Parceaud

Letter to My 11-Year-Old Self from My 60-Year-Old Self

Dear Catherine,

This afternoon, your sixth-grade teacher mocked your dreams of higher education. He asked the class who planned on attending university. A few hands eagerly shot up, including yours.

The teacher addressed students one by one to provide his assessment on whether they would achieve their goal or not. When it was your turn, he looked at you and said: 'No, you're not going to university. You'll have a couple of kids by then and you won't be going anywhere.' I remember the shock that coursed through your body in that instant. On the outside, you remained calm and didn't say a word. But internally, waves of humiliation, disbelief, confusion crashed through your little 11-year-old body. A seed of doubt was planted where, until now, confidence had flourished. Why in the world did the teacher view you in this way?

Today, I want to reassure you that you will indeed attend university. Do not pay attention to the teacher's comments. His view is not as important as he tries to make it. Granted, he is in a position of authority, but he is only a tiny blip on your journey, nothing more. Overall, I'm happy to say that you will never waver in your focus to pursue post-secondary studies. Although steep cliffs and sheer drops will appear along the way, you will not fall into the void. Forge on ahead, dear, that's what you've always done.

You went to university, Catherine. Yes, you did. You completed a first bachelor's degree. and worked in your field. Your life took a turn, you became a single parent and with a two-year-old in tow, you went back to university. You moved to a new city and completed a second bachelor's degree, this time in education. You spent a dozen rewarding years working as an elementary school teacher. To specialize in TESL, you registered to an intensive post graduate program for teachers. Later, while holding down a full-time college teacher's position, you conducted research for the thesis which led to a Master's degree in education. You continued teaching at the college level for nearly twenty years.

Post secondary education led you to many different places, stimulating people and enriching experiences. It led to a gratifying career that allowed you to flourish and touch so many lives. Catherine, you didn't attend one university, indeed you graduated from four different universities.

I'll never know why that sixth grade teacher announced you wouldn't go to university. Clearly, it was unprofessional for him to say that to a keen, bright eyed 11-year-old. There will always be individuals along the way who try to cast darkness on your light. You need to keep moving, leave them behind, stay true to yourself, and chase your dreams. That little girl has a fire burning in her that nobody and nothing can extinguish.

Take care and never stop believing in yourself.

Lots of love,

Catherine xox

Catherine Parceaud (she/her) lives in both the Lower Saint Lawrence region of Quebec and Nunavik. She is a recently retired college teacher and lung cancer survivor. The newfound freedom allows her to practice much-loved activities like walking daily in wild areas, reading, writing, sewing, and learning about all kinds of new stuff. She loves spending time outdoors with her naturalist husband, exploring, birdwatching, and fly fishing.

Marjorie Tesser

Dear Twelve-Year-Old Me,

When our parents moved I found the diary; cracked white leatherette, broken lock, no key, on which was written in blue pen, "Private! Keep Out! Do Not Read! I remember writing in it, curled over the desk in my little room or staring out the window at a lone tree, the crescent moon caught in its uppermost branches. The daily entries were brief and boring: school, the allergist, orthodontist, the library. A world where things just happened to me. The endnotes, before and after, were livelier. Privacy statements front and back (underlined, many exclamation marks, all caps)—stern admonishments not to read and if read, not to divulge. Inspirational quotes. A one-page "About The Owner: A Short Auto-Biography" (factual, formal). In the back, after New Year's Eve, a series of lists: *People I Admire, Favorite Authors, People I Had Dreams About, Magazines I Like, Movies, People I Look Like*. The longest was *Ambitions*, a list of 26 prescriptions for future activity, vocational and procedural aspirations, goals for achievements, acclaim.

I wonder if you'd be disappointed in me. I failed to *write each day in diary* in which your list was scrawled and revised (8). I didn't *become a spy* (18) or *stewardess* (3). I did not *join the circus* (4) or the *Peace Corps* (22) or *the foreign service* (25). Did not become an *actress* (7) or *a journalist* (2). *Riding school in England* (5) was not in the cards; *an English accent* (6) would not supplant my Brooklyn. My hair never *grew waist-length* (12). I didn't attend the *Ivy* I got into (17), but State. I don't *live in a castle* (15). And finally, I've somehow chosen to replicate the safe and cozy domesticity you so longed to escape.

To be frank, many of your aspirations did not turn out to suit. By the time I was a senior no one cool went *to prom with a really handsome boy* (22), or anyone. Careers that to a child appeared glamorous seem to adult me onerous. Would that I'd heeded your inspiration to *learn computer programming* (24) though!

The youngest in your grade, you were "quiet," trying to make sense of things. While allowed preferences, you hadn't yet worked out the nexus between goals and action. You didn't feel a sense of agency. You dreamed of life less circumscribed, ambitions impelled in large part by reading. In retrospect, I see that some of your aims expressed a wish to be a different kind of person, more daring, a mouth and fists instead of ears and eyes and a tendency towards compromise.

Why were you not bolder? I'm afraid the inertia that kept you static still shadows me. You whisper and I hang back, as you did, perhaps not out of shyness, but some innate reticence.

But on the whole your own natural bents have served me well. I still experience that separate self who observes, as you did; still gaze out the window at trees as if they're going to tell me something.

I didn't *write a bestseller at 14* (1); it took me nearly half a century longer to publish, but I did *become an author* (2). I have *family, husband and kids, the dog, a house* (15); do *travel* (16) and *learn languages* (19) though not to the extent you'd dreamed of. I've continued to *LEARN, period* (20); have even won some *writing contests* (13).

So maybe you'd be a little satisfied at what we've made of me, and I'll try to love you too, whose dreams, laudably, were limitless; who, as I try to, did the best she then could do.

XOX Always, Marjorie

Marjorie Tesser's (she/her) poetry and prose have appeared in Anti-Heroin Chic, Whale Road Review, Cutleaf, SWWIM, poets.org, and other journals and anthologies. Her debut full-length poetry collection, Unquiet, is forthcoming in 2027 from Cornerstone Press. The author of poetry chapbooks The Important Thing Is, *winner of the Firewheel Chapbook Award, and* The Magic Feather, *she co-edited three anthologies of poetry and prose for Demeter Press and Bowery Books, and is editor-in-chief of MER-Mom Egg Review, a literary magazine focused on motherhood. More info at https://linktr.ee/marjorietesser.*

Dory Maguire

Dear Sweet Summer Child,

I understand.

I understand your high ideals,
your sense of justice, your vantage point–
and from there,
how easy it is for everything to be fair and square.

I understand how, when family members wrong you,
betray you, belittle you,
or otherwise lose your trust,
you do not retaliate,
you do not talk behind their backs;
you simply write them out of your existence.

Dead to you,
now unable to hurt you again.
It is uncanny, unnerving,
how often you have had to use this
opposite of Día de los Muertos—
whatever this is.

From here,
as I turn fifty,
let me tell you:
they were doing the best they could
with what they had.

They were not trying to hurt you.
They were clumsy at worst.

I see them.
They are not bad, maybe misdirected.

I understand.
Someday you'll understand.

Dory Maguire (she/her) is the author of five self-published collections of poetry, each illustrated with her original photography. Dory's poems have received multiple honorable mentions in the National Federation of State Poetry Societies' annual contests and appear in several anthologies. A committed advocate for poets, Dory hosted her local poetry workshop on her patio during the pandemic when library meetings were suspended, and she remains an active presence in the poetry community, supporting small groups and gatherings both in-person and via Zoom. She lives on a horse farm in Pennsylvania, where she spends her free time sprouting trees, tending forests, and drawing inspiration from the land she stewards.

Elena Martínez-Vidal

Dear teenage Elena,

I wish that I could meet you, give you advice, and you would change. Life would be better then. Perhaps? However, looking back at your (my) upbringing, I don't think it would work.

That Baptist upbringing has it claws into you. Years of terror because you know you are going to hell. You pray and pray. God is always watching and taking stock. Oh, how deep the claws are in the flesh.

Your life is full of guilt. You can't even say you want to become a professional actor because that might be an affront to God. Your life is heavy with guilt. Anything you do or say that is "bad" will send you to hell.

Your life is a prison of guilt. While college will lessen some of the guilt, the prison bars stay thick and impenetrable. Until finally, seeing how guilt-ridden you are feeling, during a Christmas visit, your mother will give you a copy of Shirley MacLaine's book *Out on a Limb*. This book will break through the bars, unlock the door, and allow you to exhale, letting guilt slowly seep out of the body and mind. New possibilities will be seen and able to be explored. It will be a matter of growing into a future without guilt.

But, oops, all those years made you shy and hypervigilant. Having an emotionally abusive spouse won't help. That will also be a product of religious guilt. It will take years to continue shedding the religious habits of mind. And then shedding the husband with them.

But HALLELUJAH! You will do it with a little bit of help! You will grow and mature and begin to touch your potential.

I have no regrets. Know that. Everything that has happened has resulted in the here and now. And I am good! I am happy where I am now!

With lots of love and tons of hugs,

Elena

Elena Martínez-Vidal (she/her) was born in New York and spent her early years living in Pennsylvania and New Jersey before making South Carolina her home. She holds a Bachelor of Arts in Theatre and French from Dickinson College in Carlisle, Pennsylvania, and a Master of Fine Arts in Acting from the University of South Carolina in Columbia. She also completed nearly all requirements for a Master of Arts in Communication at USC and earned a Certificate in Higher Education Leadership.

Elena is a faculty member at Midlands Technical College in Columbia, where she previously served for sixteen years as Chair of the Humanities Department. In addition to her academic work, she is a professional actor and director. She also writes reflective essays and musings on Medium.

D. Nichole Davis

Dear Little Nicky,

Let me tell you something you will not understand for years.

Success has a cost.

A real one.

And sooner or later, it collects what it is owed.

You are entering adulthood with a belief that will be challenged. Right now, you believe success is earned through hard work, loyalty, and excellence. You think that if you prepare enough, show up enough, and sacrifice enough, the people in power will reward your effort. You assume that the road to achievement is fair.

It is not.

You will first learn this in your career. You will put in long days, long nights, and long seasons carrying work that should have belonged to an entire team. You will show initiative. You will solve problems. You will make yourself dependable. You will sit through meetings with a smile while quietly feeling the weight of responsibilities that were never meant for one person. You will stretch yourself thin trying to prove that you are ready for the next level.

And when the opportunity arrives, you will be passed over. More than once. Even after you gave everything you had. Even after you went above and beyond. Even after you sacrificed your time, your rest, and your peace to show you were committed.

Doing your best and still not being enough is part of the cost.

You will also learn in your personal life that some people will only celebrate you when you stay in the role they assigned you. The moment your growth challenges their comfort, they will distance themselves. You will experience friendships that feel mutual until you stop being the constant giver. You will realize that the minute your usefulness ends, some people leave without hesitation. They will act as if the bond you believed in was one-sided all along.

That cost will feel targeted, but it will also bring clarity.

Success will even demand pieces of your health. There will be seasons when you push yourself harder than you should. You will ignore your body's warnings because you want to keep up, stay relevant, stay ahead. You will convince yourself that slowing down is failure. That resting means losing ground. That saying, "I need a break," is a weakness.

Your body will disagree.

But even after your strokes, you will try to return to your old pace, because you believe grit is the only language success understands. But your recovery will force you to face a truth you spent years avoiding. Success is not sustainable if it requires you to abandon yourself. It cannot be worth risking your health, your breath, your mind, or your future. It cannot demand the very pieces of you that keep you alive.

This is where your definition of success will change.

You will learn that success is not just the promotion, the position, the platform, or the praise. True success is the ability to honor your limits without shame. True success is walking away from environments that take without giving. True success is choosing relationships rooted in reciprocity instead of expectation. True success is understanding that your health, your purpose, and your peace are not bargaining chips.

You will learn that people who misunderstand your confidence will judge you based on rumors they never bothered to verify. They will create stories about you without ever witnessing anything for themselves. You will be talked about, speculated about, and misunderstood. But you will also grow strong enough to stop caring. Because you will learn that none of those voices ever paid a single one of your costs.

And this is the wisdom you will earn.

Yes, success requires sacrifice. Yes, it costs energy, time, discipline, and resilience. But it should not cost your health. It should not cost your peace. It should not cost your identity or your worth. It should not cost relationships that were supposed to hold you up. It should not cost your joy or your ability to breathe in your own life.

Success will always cost something. But you get to decide what you refuse to pay.

One day, you will build a life defined by alignment instead of exhaustion. You will pursue goals that honor you instead of drain you. You will choose environments that see your value instead of exploiting it. You will learn that saying no is part of success, not a threat to it. You will set boundaries that protect the parts of you that success used to consume.

And most importantly, you will realize that nothing is worth achieving if you have to lose yourself to do it.

With clarity, truth, and the wisdom you earned the hard way,

Nicky

D. Nichole Davis (she/her) is a leadership strategist, attorney, and adjunct law professor with a track record of delivering high-impact, experience-driven leadership development. Drawing on her background in risk management, legal ethics, and professional responsibility, she helps leaders navigate conflict, burnout, ethical gray areas, and cultural breakdowns with clarity and credibility. After surviving three strokes, Nichole redefined leadership through the lens of resilience, accountability, and human-centered decision-making. She is the founder of D. Nichole Davis Consulting and the creator of the Experience-Driven Leadership framework, equipping organizations to move from reflection to measurable, sustainable impact.

Mare Schumacher

You will be fine with no gall bladder.
You will be fine with no gall bladder and one breast.
You will be fine with no gall bladder, one breast, and metal in your wrist.
You will be fine with no gall bladder, one breast, metal in your wrist, and three fractured ribs.
If only I could go back to 2021, the year I lost the aforementioned breast, I would have some advice for my 63-year-old self...

Dear Younger Self,

This year, you will be diagnosed with breast cancer.

It is going to be quite the surprise. It won't fit the decades-long breast exam pattern you know so well. Usually, you go to your annual mammogram, then you get a letter that says a) "Looks good, see you next year!" or b) "Come back for an ultrasound, your dense breast tissue may be hiding something." If it's the latter, you get an ultrasound and the doc comes out after reviewing it and says, "Looks good, see you next year!"

This time, you will know something is wrong when the script diverges from the usual. This time, when the ultrasound is over, the doc will walk in and sit down. You will think, "*Uh oh.* The doctor doesn't usually *sit down.*" Your heart will sink. You will want to put your fingers on the doctor's lips and say, "Don't speak!" The doc is supposed to *stand* there and say, "Looks good. See you next year!" and leave. Instead, she will point out two masses on the screen (which your sisters Nancy and Martha will later name "Thing 1" and "Thing 2"). They are in the same breast, four centimeters apart. This rules out a lumpectomy and you will need a mastectomy. A mastectomy will get it over with quickly, people will tell you that mastectomies are like car washes these days: drive in by 8:00, pre-op, remove breast, post-op, drive out by 5:00.

Despite the easy-in, easy-out surgery, being diagnosed with cancer will make you think about death. About all of those who've died of breast cancer, about breast cancer walks, pink ribbons, and people in movies who die slow deaths. In the movies, the person with cancer slowly deteriorates, first losing their hair, then their energy, then their life force. Almost always in the movies, the cancer diagnosis and impending death coincides with our hero's emotional journey—making peace with their mother (*Terms of Endearment*), letting themselves fall in love (*The Fault in Our Stars*), or perhaps rekindling bonds with their old gangster friends for one last heist (I think I made that one up).

For you, it may be the first time in your adult life that you feel truly vulnerable. Your partner, Luis, has been in an existential crisis ever since he was born, but you rarely think about dying at all. Now you will have to reckon with it. It will make you more wary of things, a little more afraid, but at the same time it will give you a desire to enjoy life now, while you can, because it is going to end sometime and it may be sooner than you think.

There is the death part, then there is a loss of a body part part. Losing any part of your body is creepy and feels sort of *wrong*, and losing a breast will be more problematic than losing a gall bladder. You've always had a complicated relationship with your breasts. On one hand, you saw breasts as mostly unnecessary appendages—dead weight, really, unless you are going to use them for breastfeeding, a worthy cause, but not a cause you were pursuing. As a kid, you thought women couldn't run and you concluded it must be the breasts. The day would come when you would unwillingly obtain breasts and wouldn't race around in your sneakers, untethered and unfettered any more. On the other hand, you grew to really like the size and shape of your breasts (if you must say so yourself) and how they looked in a turtleneck, at least by some standards of beauty. There is the sensual part of breasts, of course, which is very nice. Most importantly, you learned that you can run, jump, repel, swing, leap, and do many things even if you *have breasts*! In fact, you will do so many of these things that you'll break your arm and some ribs while you are hiking and biking.

Death, breasts, reckoning: you will have a lot to process. What you'll need to do is research the heck out of this, just like you do when you're looking for a hotel or finding the best way to get dog vomit out of carpet. That is always your best coping mechanism. You will know that you can't control everything (or anything) by researching, but you will feel more secure because you've walked through all of the possibilities, looked down all of the avenues. What type of cancer do you have? (The kind that is "fed" by hormones, the most common.) What are your chances of surviving this kind of cancer? (High.) What are the odds you could get cancer in the other breast? (Low.) What medications are recommended? (Hormone suppressors.) What diet is best? (Eat more vegetables. Duh.)

On the day of the mastectomy, you'll be nervous, with butterflies in your stomach. You should be comfortable, so remember to wear sweatpants, your Dunder Mifflin t-shirt, and the horse socks that say "giddy-up" because the surgeon loves horses too. By the time Patty, who is clearly a veteran of operating room procedures, pushes you on the gurney expertly through the operating room doors, your heart will be in your throat. Patty will announce to the team members in the OR, "This is Mary, but she goes by Mare." Without missing a beat, Allison will introduce herself as "Al", Cindy as "Sin" and Patty as "Pat." You will be in good hands. Make sure to tell the anesthesiologist that you are a lightweight, so he gives you the proper dose. In seconds, the anesthesia will make you feel really good.

You will see the operating lights dissolve into sunshine. The butterflies will be out of your stomach and flying all around you. You float along on your horse, hair flowing behind you. You'll be joined by the rest of the women you know, some in the lead and some behind. You will look over your shoulder and cry, "¡Adios, tumors!" as you float over the Ponderosa Pines and red rocks.

When it is all over, you will cross the threshold into a new world of women you haven't known before. You will be blanketed by the warmth of a whole world of breast cancer survivors. A survivor will only be a stranger until the moment you share your stories with each other. Then she will become a friend and supporter. And you, in turn, will become part of this world, helping others when they are diagnosed and want to talk to someone. Your sister Nancy will get breast cancer next year (maybe just to get the attention away from you), and you will be there for her. Nothing lifts you up as much as lifting up others. COVID-19 will be in full-swing, and you, like all epidemiologists, will be badly needed on the front lines for the heavy lifting there. You will get back to work as soon as possible to help. No time for futzing around with cancer.

You will break your arm two months after the breast surgery and refuse a donation of meals because it is too embarrassing to start a new "meal train" two months after the last one. There is a big narrow scar where your left breast used to be, but the prosthesis (that's a fake breast) and bras they will give you will make it impossible to tell there is anything missing. It will feel sort of numb around the scar like it had Novocain shot into it. It will feel this way for years. But the effect of all this on your brain is the opposite of numbing. You will start to put more significance on the present, living not *entirely* in the moment, but much more for now.

One in eight American women will get breast cancer in their lifetimes. It will just be your turn. And you, my younger self, will be fine.

Mare Schumacher (she/her) is a writer, storyteller, STEAM advocate, hiker, traveler, and epidemiologist living in Flagstaff, Arizona, with her unruly 2.5 dogs and husband. In 2024, she won a Moth StorySLAM and went on to win the Moth GrandSLAM in Ann Arbor, Michigan, her hometown.

Letters of Celebration

You were light long before you knew it,
and I am still carrying your glow.

-Tisha Marie Fritz

A. Laura Brody

A little story, just for you, to remind you of how brave you were then and continue to be...

She waited nervously, lingering after school.

In the morning she had loaded her book bag with the heaviest art books she could carry and brought them with her to kindergarten. She was already flustered from having to go to the older kids' classroom for reading. The books in her class were boring. She preferred the books in the bigger classrooms, but she didn't know anyone there. She was so much smaller than the other kids and sometimes they frightened her.

She didn't really have friends. Her family had moved to the tiny town for a university job only that year. It was a part time job and her father worked for a food packing company the rest of the time, preparing produce for the Jolly Green Giant. Her step mother worked at an office, but where was unclear. They were not around that often.

The girl's job was to go to school, take care of her younger brother and sister, and to read them to sleep. She tried her best but always seemed to get things wrong, and was punished or blamed for the family's problems. She did not understand why.

When the bigger boys laughed at her and hit her head into the metal mailbox on the way home from school, at first she tried to hide it from her family. Surely somehow this would turn out to be her fault, like so many things were at home. But eventually the story came out and her stepmother said she would teach the girl to fight. "If all else fails, keep heavy books in your bag and whack them with it."

This time, the girl did just that.

The boys scattered. They were unused to having anyone fight back. It wasn't until much later when the family learned that they were 5th and 6th graders, banding together to beat up on a little girl.

All the girl knew was that those boys never bothered her again.

XO Laura

A. Laura Brody turns wheelchairs, walkers, and mobility scooters into works of art and transforms reclaimed materials, giving them new lives. She is the founder and curator of Opulent Mobility, an international exhibit that celebrates disability in all its forms. www.opulentmobility.com www.dreamsbymachine.com

Dr. Lynn A. Volkenant

I will be there for you, even when things seem hopeless.

Dear Small Lynn,

Do you remember when you first learned to read, on your father's lap? You were only four years old when you began noticing how words fit together on the page to make a story. Your dad read from all four *Winnie the Pooh* books every night before bed. One story or one poem was never enough, and as you trudged up the stairs in your pajamas with feet, you tried to hold all those pictures and words in your head to mull them over before sleeping. In bed you pretended to sleep while imagining Pooh getting his head stuck in a honey jar. Under the fuzzy green bedspread, you whispered, "Oh bother, you silly old bear." It was then your dad started calling you Lynnie the Pooh.

That was when you told your friend that nobody could see, (Mr. Nobododdy) that you wanted to become a library when you grew up. No, not a librarian, because librarians could only hold a few stories at a time in their hands. You wanted to be a library because then you could hold all the books in the world in your arms forever. Not just any library either, you wanted to be the big library in New York that your parents took you to see. The one with the gigantic stone lions in front of it. The one with fifty million books, maps, charts, and photos in it. The one that has a reading room named after a flower. The one that keeps the first Winnie the Pooh toys and books that are scruffed up because Christopher Robin loved them so much.

As you grew older, your love of reading grew with you. Every time you went to the public library in St. Paul (which does not have lions) you checked out ten books and read them all in a week. You read outside on the bench your dad built beneath the big tree in the backyard. You tucked stories inside your social studies books so it would look like you were studying. Almost every night you snuck into the bathroom after being tucked in and read for hours perched on the cold commode.

You became Charlotte in *Charlotte's Web;* you were Mary Lennox in *The Secret Garden* and Jo in *Little Women*. You even read the backs of cereal boxes. Nothing could make you stop. One day in grade four when you went home for lunch, you went upstairs to read for just a minute... and when your mother found you two hours later, she startled you by yelling "Why are you still here, you are so late for going back to school." Even though you sobbed in terror all the three blocks to your classroom, you could not stop loving books.

Now you are an old woman who reads every day, and your 95-year-old dad still calls you Miss Pooh. Miss Lynnie the Pooh. Dr. Lynnie the Pooh. "Oh bother, that silly old bear."

Lynn Volkenant (she/her) is a retired educator and author who has happily been surrounded by children for most of her life. She left the frozen landscape of Minnesota five years ago and immigrated to Charleston, South Carolina, where it is much warmer. She lives there with her husband Michael and little dog Beatrice. She loves to read and write and is currently working on a memoir entitled Little Bare Feet on the Floor. In it, she visits her own upbringing and memorializes the years she spent as the mom of five boys.

Rumaisa Reza

You Built Yourself, Piece by Piece

Dear Younger Me,

Do you remember those late afternoons—the ones you spent waiting on the floor, tiny fingers sorting colors and shapes, building houses and stories out of Lego bricks? You didn't know it then, but every small creation was you learning how to build yourself, one piece at a time. Back then, those hours were enough, weren't they? Enough to make you feel like the whole world was yours just because you could build something out of nothing but imagination.

You called yourself dumb, the least clever one in the family, but you were never empty. You were full. Full of emotion, full of soundless dreams, full of the kind of depth no one had words for yet. You learned to hide those feelings like secrets no one deserved to see. You thought silence was your safest shield, that if no one knew, nothing could hurt you.

But I'm here now, your future self, and I want you to know something: The things you hid to protect yourself were the things that made you whole.

Your fears—of failing, of not being enough, of losing what little you had—were never your weakness. Even when they shook you, even when they made you feel small, they also taught you how to take pain and turn it into something, into writing, into love, into softness, into you.

I know what you're thinking... that everything feels like a test you're always failing. That you'll always be the one who's behind, the one no one believes, not even the ones you love most. I know those nights when you cried quietly just so you wouldn't disappoint the people who called your sadness "overthinking." And I know how hard it was when the only two friends you ever had in your life, your mother and father, misunderstood you, didn't believe your truth.

But I also know this: you survived. And not by chance, but by choice.

You chose writing when speaking hurt. You chose to care when anger was easier. You chose to love someone who taught you how to see the world through kindness. That boy you met—the one who made you feel things you never felt before—that feeling was real, and it shaped you. It wasn't childish, it wasn't a waste and it wasn't everything you thought. It was a small beginning. The first bloom in a long, strange spring.

And yes, you let him go. You thought freeing him would free you from the hurt. But here's the truth; letting go didn't erase him. It grew something inside you, the type of tenderness that wouldn't exist if you hadn't felt deeply in the first place. You didn't ruin anything, I promise. You just learned how heavy love can feel even when it's no longer there.

So here's what I want to tell you about the future: You won't become perfect. You won't stop failing. You won't find all the answers.

But you will learn how to stay for yourself. You will learn how to talk to your own heart. You will learn how to forgive yourself for all the mistakes that seemed unforgivable. You will learn that your sensitivity is a strength, that feeling everything so intensely is why you write with such softness and truth. You will learn how to love yourself, of course not instantly or magically, but slowly and surely, through forgiveness and grace.

And one day, you'll stop asking who you *should* be and start accepting who you already *are*. You will live your life in ways you never planned, but that's okay. Your life was never meant to follow a map anyways. It was always meant to feel like a story.

Every human has different seasons and so did you. No one stays the same. The thing is those seasons may or may not repeat. And nowhere does winter stay forever, neither does grief.

So I'll end this the way I wish someone had spoken to you then: You matter.

Every version of you matters. The one who cried. The one who stayed quiet. The one who loved too much, felt too much. Also the one who let go too soon. And every version of you is still here, breathing, building a life out of colors and shapes you once thought were broken.

Trust this: the pain will not leave, but it will make room for something gentler. You don't know it yet, but there are a lot of things waiting for you. They might not seem really great or magical at the very first, but trust me, they will take you somewhere better.

Trust them. Trust yourself.

I am really so proud of you, more than you ever believed you deserved.

With all the love you never knew you needed,

Your Future Self

Save your favorite Lego pieces. You'll need reminders of how you used to build worlds.

Rumaisa Reza (she/her) is a writer from Bangladesh, drawn to intimate, reflective storytelling. Their work often centers on memory, self-understanding, and quiet moments of emotional reclamation.

Dr. Alicia P. Harris

Hey Girl Hey!

As I have walked out this life and spent 55 years circling the sun, there are some things I believe I owe you in terms of advice, support, encouragement and empowerment. I have taken the time to interrogate my thoughts, decisions, and actions during this life journey and I have this to say to you.

You are stronger than you think, you have accomplished tremendous things, your future is bright, and you control the narrative. Do not allow someone else to write your story! Although they may be a character or circumstance in the pages of your life story, YOU are the leading lady. You carry the plot as well as engage the audience, the world is your audience! The stage you occupy will be one of great recognition but will come with the need for discernment as some people will only be around for the ride that benefits them. Take your liberty in terms of casting changes, adding what and who is needed and removing that which no longer serves you. Afford yourself grace when life dictates that you pivot.

Remember your dreams of becoming a doctor? You spent many days allowing your imagination to take you into the operating room and your dolls were the patients. With continuous practice you extricated foreign objects and gave invisible sutures, all while nursing your dolls back to health. Your mother believed in your dreams so much that she began enrolling you in gifted and talented classes on Saturdays as well as exposing you to as many opportunities that fed your desire to work in medicine. Unfortunately, the pull of the world was much stronger than your desire to become a surgeon and before you know it, the concrete jungle you called home attempted to swallow you. Your decisions were not always the best and your yearning for acceptance, love and a sense of belonging landed you in some toxic and at times abusive relationships. However, things do turn around and guess what? You do become a doctor but not a surgeon. You become one that can cut into the negative mindsets and emotional dysregulation of others, helping them to become the best versions of themselves. Your life's work will be that of women's empowerment, giving voice to those who felt they either had no voice or were unsure how to use theirs. You will be acknowledged on large platforms for the work you do in your community and your own personal story of perseverance and determination will reach thousands.

Another tremendous accomplishment you will experience is the birth and raising of three epic children. Unfortunately, you will take the journey of motherhood as a single parent, which I know is the opposite of your dreams of having a loving two-parent home complete with a dog. You won't get everything right with them, but you will work hard to provide guidance, protection and nurturing that will carry over to your beautiful grandchildren. Life will be challenging as a single mom. Decisions about finances will be tough, you will experience homelessness and it will feel like the weight of the world is on your shoulders. However, those three beautiful, rambunctious children are depending on you and in their eyes, you will be Superwoman! There will be times that you feel like a failure, but I promise you that all that life throws your way will be building blocks that contribute to the woman you will become. Keep your head up, dry your tears and be kind to the woman staring back at you in the mirror. Even in the midst of verbal and physical abuse, you manage to instill goodness, kindness and courage into your children which will be passed on for generations to come. Your children will grow up and bless you by being productive, influential citizens in society. You have done the very best that you could and your children will have the utmost respect and admiration for you.

Refuse to allow betrayal, abandonment, abuse, and discouragement to impede your ability to shine brightly. Let go of grudges against those who failed to protect you, support you and teach you how to navigate life in a healthy way and always celebrate your accomplishments no matter how small. Use your voice for good, first with yourself and then on behalf of others. You are a powerful force to be reckoned with and although you may not believe that initially, you will grow into a warrior that is unstoppable.

Dream BIG! Laugh LOUD! Love HARD! Believe in yourself with every fiber of your being. Speak up and speak out to make your needs known, your presence matters. Allow others to be there to meet them. Do not be distracted by what you see and hear, you are enough! No one can take what you don't give them. Understand that it is ok when people walk away in fact, be thankful for them doing so as it allows you to make room for the ones who will stay by your side.

Lean on God, trust Him, follow Him, focus on Him and pace yourself. Use your energy wisely and remember your loved ones who have gone on before you and now cheer you on as you run your race. Do not forfeit the blessings on your life and remember, you were never meant to be MEDIOCRE!

Love you girlie,

Dr. Alicia P. Harris

Alicia Patricia Harris is a native of Paterson, NJ, where she graduated from the infamous Eastside High School under the leadership of Principal Joe Clark. Dr. Harris is a Licensed Professional Counselor and supervisor, as well as a Licensed Addictions Counselor, and has worked in these fields for over 10 years. She obtained her Ph.D. from the University of the Cumberlands in Wilmington, KY, in Counselor Education and Supervision, and her mission is to assist individuals in the pursuit of positive mental health.

Dr. Harris is the Founder and CEO of Pieces a Soulful Journey with Alopecia and the visionary of the BeYoutiFull Movement, which focuses on self-love and self-acceptance, encouraging women to show up authentically, embracing all of who they are. Dr. Harris has been featured in articles written by multiple digital magazines and is devoted to community service, advocacy, spreading education and awareness around Alopecia. She is known as the Alopecia Warrior!

Jenn Laurenza

Someday you will be free to know who you are.

It is 1993 and you are in eleventh grade when you are introduced in English class to the controversial British writer, E.M. Forster (praise God that your fundamentalist, Pentecostal parents let you attend public school). You are savvy enough to hide your new obsession with his book Maurice, about a closeted gay man in early 20th century England. You secure a copy of the movie (most likely at the library, your favorite place) and watch it secretly in the basement family room of your home with no one around, standing in front of the television in case you need to shut off the VCR quickly. You are not sure how you even knew there was a movie version of the book or how to find it, but you had a way of finding things you were meant to find.

In an essay about this book, you write in support of same-sex relationships, which surprises you because it is not a position you even knew you had. In '90s rural America, this position is not acceptable. It is definitely not acceptable in your family or your church community; gay people are equated with pedophiles and are not permitted to work with children in Sunday School, Children's Church, or the childcare room if they ever "struggled" with homosexuality.

You recall writing this memorable essay only after you realize your English teacher, Mr.Tripp, will keep your secret support of gay people safe. You have a keen eye for these things and a sixth sense that helps you size people up with precision. Mr. Tripp, who might be your guardian angel, looks a little like Jesus with his flowing long hair, scruffy beard, and simple, wholesome clothing, except he is white and very blonde. He lives on a sheep farm and makes things (clothes? blankets?) out of wool. Still, you write the essay in secret and hide it in your desk drawer under piles of other papers. You discover it well into adulthood, after coming out as a lesbian at 33, and it makes you cry.

You stop writing in your 20s, too busy with graduate school, jobs, and babies. But you dream of making art in the form of words. It will seem like a long time—until after your kids are teenagers—but you will write again. You will become a better writer and will even go back to school for creative nonfiction (who knew there was such a thing?). You will learn with like-minded students and it will be hard and sometimes triggering but you will love it, nonetheless. And you will tell the truth and no one will be able to take that from you, because it's your story.

Someday you will be free to love who you want.

You will think you know love at 19, when you marry your high school boyfriend. He makes spreadsheets of the timeline of your life together, without your input, and provides you a weekly allowance. You will lose all sense of yourself, who you are, and what you want, but you actually never knew that anyway. After 13 years of marriage, when you are 33, you will find the courage to leave him and begin dating women, which you knew you should have done from the very beginning, but couldn't.

Three years later, after heartbreak with your first girlfriend, you will experience true love with a woman named Mary (an unfortunate name for a lesbian marrying an ex-evangelical) and you will marry her. You will find true happiness with her—her easy smile, infectious laugh, and adventurous spirit make you feel complete, as codependent as that sounds (and maybe is). This love will be so sweet and pure—sandwiched in between the irritation and annoyance that comes with marriage—that you will fear its end, through death or demise, every day. You will love her so much that you will agree to add two more children to your family. That makes five children. The stress of five children, especially two adoptive children with trauma histories and significant behavior problems, will nearly send you over the edge, but love between you and Mary keeps you safely cocooned.

Someday you will be free to believe what you want.

When you are in your 30s, you won't worry so much about going to hell because you will know that hell is an imaginary place that was created to scare people into conformity, like the sign says on the evangelical church down the street from where you live now: "Choose Jesus or get on the highway to hell." Someday you won't worry anymore that Jesus is coming to take you "home," like you did when you were 12, deathly afraid each night in your bed wrapped in a yellow comforter with tiny white flowers, that the rapture was imminent and the next day could be your last (if you were "saved" enough to be raptured, that is).

Someday you will still care what people think, but you will care less.

It will never stop hurting to be rejected or to have your parents or friends be ashamed of you because you are gay, but this will hurt less over time. By the time you have reached your fifth decade, you will know this in your bones even if it causes heartache. In your 40s, you won't be able to remember the last time your parents told you they were proud of you, but somehow, you will still know that you are ok–with or without their support or unconditional love.

You will seek your own spirituality that sometimes includes Christianity and sometimes does not.

You will turn toward Buddhism, Humanism, Paganism, and Atheism at times, but the pull to return to a Christian church will always remain strong. For you, church is like a second family, one that provides a sense of purpose, community, and belonging. The little yellow church where you get married the second time, by Reverend Patty with her butch haircut and rainbow scarf, will never lose its sweetness, no matter how ungodly and vile Christianity (and its followers) seem at times.

Someday the brevity of life will astound and terrify you and you will choose life anyway, despite everything.

Life will seem to whiz by at times and you will feel like you have wasted time not allowing yourself to embrace your sexuality earlier in life. Before you know what has happened, you will be in your 40s staring at middle age, seeking answers beyond eternal life. At 48, you will still be searching for your place in the world and a sense of belonging, just like you were at 12 and 18 and 33. But you will be wiser, which helps.

Someday you will be free to know who you are. And who you are is not only good enough; it is imperfect and beautiful.

Jenn Laurenza (she/her) is a wife, mother, writer, and Licensed Mental Health Counselor with a thriving group practice of psychotherapists. She specializes in women's and LGBTQ mental health and is an advocate for the LGBTQ community and other marginalized populations. As a therapist, she strives to help people live meaningful and authentic lives. She has published an essay on parenting teens and co-authored a chapter in a graduate textbook on systemic influences impacting the counseling of children and adolescents. She mostly writes for self-preservation, healing, and creative expression, although she wishes she could write for a living and still pay the mortgage! Jenn lives in southeastern Massachusetts with her wife, children, three dogs, and four cats.

Tisha Marie Fritz

Hey Love,

If I could run back to this day, I would go joyfully.

I can see you in that parking lot, still laughing with your brother, still full of that confident, eager light.

I would scoop you up and tell you everything you needed to hear but never got in the ways you deserved.

You are pure light, little one. You do not know that yet, but the light you carry is real. It is the kind that makes people pause. It is the kind that softens a room. It is the kind that is sacred, even when others do not treat it that way.

The world will try to dim it and confuse you. It will make you wonder if you are too much or not enough. I want you to know you are already exactly who you are meant to be.

I see how you hold your brother close. I see how you try to keep him safe even though you are the one who should be protected.

That is who you are.

A watcher. A feeler. A girl who knew how to care long before she knew how to name it. You learned to survive by being good, by being kind, by studying every room like it had rules you needed to learn fast.

You carry that still. And here is the truth you needed back then. You do not have to earn love. You already are, Love.

There will be people who misunderstand you.

They will call your excitement too much. They will call your big ideas unrealistic. They will try to take the shine off your imagination. Keep all of it. That energy is not a flaw. It is your first set of wings.

The girl in the pirate blouse is not pretending. She is practicing

courage. She is standing in the middle of an ordinary moment without knowing she is building a future voice that will one day steady itself and speak truth with clarity and strength.

You will not get to keep everyone you love. Loss will come early and it will come hard. But you will carry them with you. Their love and their laughter will travel with you as you grow. One day, you will write them home. You will do it with honesty and compassion, and it will matter.

If you can, when you walk across that street tonight, slow down. Feel the cool air on your cheeks. Listen to your brother's laugh. Smell the church dinner waiting inside. Let yourself enjoy it. You deserve joy that does not require anything from you.

I love you. I am proud of you. And even now, I am still becoming you.

With everything I have,

Me, age 39
Writing to age 11 me

Tisha Marie Fritz is a writer and storyteller whose work explores healing, motherhood, faith, resilience, and the hard-won beauty of becoming. Drawing from a life shaped by hardship, love, loss, and restoration, she writes to tell the truth about what breaks us, what carries us, and what helps us begin again. Her work speaks to women finding their voice, honoring their story, and choosing hope for what comes next.

Photo courtesy of author.

Post Script

And now, it could be your turn to write that letter.

It can be a difficult thing to do. A decade ago, I was not yet part of the #whatshesaidproject, but I was on this anthology journey. I was in therapy, trying to make sense of my younger years. That has been a long process. What I want you to know is that framing and reframing our narratives can be a powerful thing, and this letter writing tool is one that I have found to be effective.

I owe the nugget of this idea in part to my childhood friend, Hannah Logan. Hannah challenged me to join her in a twelve-step program for adult children of dysfunctional families. I first heard this phrase there, that we are to *parent our inner child.* Hannah seemed to be able to do this, crafting monologues of conversations between her present self and her toddler self or adolescent self or teenage self. I struggled.

Later, during nine months of weekly private sessions with therapist Caisey Hutto, I walked through the steps of *cognitive processing therapy,* and a similar task was presented. *What do I wish someone would have done for me*? Caisey asked one day. *I wish I had been treated as precious*. I answered. *What makes you feel precious?* I stumbled over my words when she asked this. I didn't have an answer. Yet.

I have since found answers to that question, and I have begun to toy with this thing, *parenting my inner child*. It is not all about traumas and recovery, though. It is about the everyday, too. It is about not only witnessing and reclaiming, but also about blessing and celebration.

During each of our workshops held in conjunction with this anthology, I wrote along with our participants. I remember vividly sitting at my kitchen table that fourth evening, scribbling out a few words from the prompt for that night and rewriting viciously this one statement.

I love her. I love her. I love her.

You can take this activity and practice the crafts of writing. You can work on creating vivid imagery, practice balancing scene with exposition, and revise prepositions and tenses and point of view. But what Shannon and I want most for you, if you take on this task, is that you find your way home–to loving yourself well.

We are not therapists. But we have become community builders. And we have plans for more workshops and more anthologies. Perhaps you'll join us.

Melanie McGehee

www.ingramcontent.com/pod-product-compliance
Lightning Source LLC
La Vergne TN
LVHW051002080826
845145LV00009B/2415

* 9 7 8 1 9 7 0 0 3 0 1 7 4 *